Helping
Children Grieve

Helping Children Grieve

When Someone They Love Dies

REVISED EDITION

Theresa M. Huntley

Augsburg Books
MINNEAPOLIS

HELPING CHILDREN GRIEVE
When Someone They Love Dies

Large-quantity purchases or custom editions of this book are available at a discount from the publisher. For more information, contact the sales department at Augsburg Fortress, Publishers, 1-800-328-4648, or write to: Sales Director, Augsburg Fortress, Publishers, P.O. Box 1209, Minneapolis, MN 55440-1209.

Cover art from Corbis Images
Cover and book design by Jessica A. Klein

Library of Congress Cataloging-in-Publication Data
Huntley, Theresa, 1961–
   Helping children grieve: when someone they love dies / Theresa M. Huntley.—
Rev. ed.
     p.cm.
   Includes bibliographical references.
   ISBN 0-8066-4265-3 (alk. paper)
   1. Children and death. 2. Grief in children. 3. Bereavement in children.
4. Children—Counseling of. I. Title.
BF723.D3 H86 2002
155.9'37'083—dc21   2002022249

The paper used in this publication meets the minimum requirements of American National Standard for Information Sciences—Permanence of Paper for Printed Library Materials, ANSI Z329.48-1984. ♾ ™

Manufactured in the U.S.A.   AF 9-4265

06   05   04   3   4   5   6   7   8   9   10

To Molly,
a special friend,
whose courage and strength
have been a source
of great inspiration
in my life.

Contents

Author's Note on Terminology

*F*or ease in reading and writing, throughout most of this book I will address the reader as the child's parent or primary caretaker, and also as if you have recently experienced the death of a loved one. I will also reference the child as a female. In doing this there is no intention on my part to suggest that one gender is more or less important than the other. I am confident that despite these syntactical choices, the material in this book can be readily applied in other circumstances.

Part 3 of the book is addressed primarily to professional caregivers in clinical or hospital settings. This material, however, is also of value to parents, families, and friends of children who are dying.

Introduction

Adults instinctively want to protect children from pain, to somehow shield them from the difficulties that life will inevitably hold for them. There is often a tendency to avoid discussing death, if at all possible. Once a death occurs, however, it becomes obvious that avoidance simply isn't possible. There comes a time when even the most difficult issues must be faced.

Rather than attempting to hide death from children, it is my firm belief that we need to explore the concept with them in a safe, non-threatening manner—a process that can begin at a very early age. Ideally, such an approach will enable children to understand death as a natural part of life rather than as a frightening occurrence that is to be dreaded.

Children are aware of their world and what is happening in it. With or without access to information regarding the death, when a loved one dies, children experience the separation that accompanies it. How they are able to understand

and cope with the loss will be influenced by the support and guidance available to them. If they have had the opportunity to learn about death prior to the loss of someone close to them, children will be better prepared for the grieving process.

Teaching children about death is not an easy task. Some people choose—either intentionally or unintentionally—not to instruct children about the concept. They assume that if children aren't talking about it, they must not be thinking about it. Given that you are reading this book, my hunch is that you realize this is not true. For whatever reason, you have decided to face the challenge of teaching children about death and are seeking information that will assist you in this endeavor.

This book is intended for everyone who interacts with children on a regular basis. You may be the child's parent, grandparent, or other extended relative, or you may be their teacher, minister, faith formation teacher, childcare provider, neighbor, or friend. Whatever the case, it is fortunate for the child that you have recognized the importance of helping her learn about the life cycle.

As you prepare to help your child, know that it will be important for you to begin by taking some time to reflect on your own thoughts and feelings related to death. You may have already experienced the death of a number of people in your life, or this may be the first significant death that you have had to face. Whatever the situation, whatever your history, if you are to help your child, self-awareness is critical. Consider what you think of death in general, as well as how you view your own mortality. Is death a source of fear and anxiety for you? Do you dread it? Does death have an element of mystery that intrigues you? Do you perceive it as part of the cycle of life, which has a beginning as well as an end, both of which are necessary in the natural order of things? Ponder these questions and become familiar with your thoughts and feelings.

Children are naturally inquisitive about all that life presents to them. If we have taken time to reflect, we will be in a better position to address children's questions openly and honestly as they occur. On the other hand, if we are unaware of our feelings, we will be unprepared to answer the questions and to deal with the feelings that arise when children confront us. Children are astute. They can often "read" our communication, both the spoken and unspoken, in our tone of voice, facial expression, and posture. Although we may be saying one thing, our nonverbal signals may be sending a contradictory message. Children will pick up on this, which can make them confused and unsure. And they may decide it's not okay to seek assistance from you, intuitively choosing instead to approach someone they feel more comfortable with.

It will also be important for you to take special care of yourself during this difficult time. Your child is grieving and so are you. In helping children face their grief, you are also making a commitment to deal with your own. You are on this journey together. You will go wherever it leads.

Consider how you have coped with difficult experiences in the past. What was helpful to you and what was not? Realize that now is probably not the time to take on new behaviors. In a time of crisis, people tend to rely on that which is familiar, regardless of whether or not it is beneficial to them. Try to draw upon your previous strengths as best you can. In doing so, you will be better equipped to meet the needs of your child. You will also be modeling the importance of self-care.

My purpose in writing this book is to help increase your awareness of how children understand and experience death. I will also offer guidance as you assist your child in grieving the loss of a loved one, or as you help your child prepare for his or her own impending death. This book is comprehensive in that it discusses the needs of all children, including those who are bereaved, those who are learning in general about the concept of death, and those who are themselves dying. The book is divided into three sections that can be read from the beginning to the end, or you can choose those parts that are most useful at a particular time. As a means of illustrating the material, I will share stories drawn from my experience as a nurse and a social worker during the past sixteen years. To protect the privacy of people involved, names and circumstances have been changed.

May your efforts be rewarded as you undertake the challenge of teaching your child about the cycle of life.

Part One
Children and Death

1
How Children
Understand Death

In this chapter, I will discuss how children understand death, particularly from a developmental perspective. This overview may provide you with a general sense of what your child might be thinking.

Children gradually develop a concept of death directly related to their age. Their understanding is also influenced by other factors, such as previous life experiences, emotional maturity, psychological development, coping abilities and style, culture and ethnicity, environment, and parental attitudes. This discussion will focus on the child's understanding primarily as it relates to age.

Specific patterns of thinking and behaving are unique to children at different stages in their development. Although many of these characteristics overlap, we can divide these stages into five distinct groups: 1) children less than three years of age, 2) children three to six years of age, 3) children six to ten years of age, 4) children ten to twelve years of age, and 5) children twelve to eighteen years of age.

These ranges are approximations and should be used only as guides. Your child is an individual and her grief will be influenced, as previously mentioned, by a number of other factors. Your child's situation is unique and must be assessed accordingly.

Children Less than Three Years of Age

Although children this age do not have the ability to understand the concept of death, they are able to respond to the experience of it in their lives. Infants and toddlers depend heavily on their parents. As a result, they worry most about separation. For them, dying means separation.

Infants have the task of learning to differentiate between themselves and their environment. As part of this task, they gradually develop a sense of being versus nonbeing. By approximately three months of age, healthy infants are secure enough to begin experimenting with these contrasting states through games such as peek-a-boo. This game provides a safe opportunity for infants to experience both fear and delight. At first the baby responds with wide eyes when the other "player" disappears from view. Then, delighted coos follow as they make eye contact with the suddenly reappearing smiling face.

During the highchair age, infants and toddlers play games of disappear and return, dropping objects from their trays and waiting for someone to retrieve them. Children are delighted to have the objects reappear and will repeat the activity over and over again. With time, however, they begin to realize that not all things come back. Rather, they are "all gone."

As children begin to appreciate "all-goneness," they will continue to experiment with the concept through game playing. These situations will produce curiosity and sometimes even fear, and can include such actions as flushing objects down the toilet, blowing out a candle, switching a light on and off repeatedly, and watching as the bath water swirls down the drain. Each of these activities helps toddlers to further understand the difference between the state of being and nonbeing.

Children Three to Six Years of Age

Children in this age group view the world from the perspective of their own experiences. Although they may use the words *die* and *dead,* they cannot truly comprehend what they have not yet experienced. In addition, their vocabulary—although expanding—is also limited. As a result, preschoolers rely on what they learn from their parents and other adults, their peers, their environment, books, television, and movies.

During this early phase in their development, children seem to regard death mainly as separation, a departure. It is clear to them that the dead are not here with us. For the preschooler, any separation, or even the prospect of one—particularly from a parent—may produce anxiety. These children may not be able to differentiate between what will be a short absence versus a long or permanent one. Therefore, it is helpful to tell children in terms they can relate to when you will be returning. You might say, for example, "Daddy is going to a meeting and will be home after your nap" or "Mommy is going to work and will pick you up before dinner." In doing this, you are helping children to become aware of, and comfortable with, the numerous little separations that are a part of life.

Preschoolers believe death is reversible. For young children to understand the finality of death, they would need to be able to recognize themselves as separate from their parents, capable of existing without them. This is beyond what they can imagine. They are dependent and know they need protection. Death, then, is viewed as temporary. People may die, but they will come back.

Although parents and other adults may tell them that death is permanent, other influences in the children's world can contradict this notion. For example, television cartoons constantly present children with life-unto-death-unto-life dynamics as characters appear to die but then spring back to life. They may also see shows or movies in which a character dies, only to see the same actor reappear later in another show.

Children this age also have difficulty imagining the reality of the radical change brought about by death. Although they may recognize that one's condition has changed—just as it does, for example, when one is sleeping—young children do not understand that the functions of the body have come to a complete stop. This is evidenced by the questions preschoolers ask. They want to know such things as: How will he eat and drink? Where will he go to the bathroom? How will he see? How will he be able to breathe? What if it smells? What will it feel like? Will he know where he is and what is happening?

Magical thinking and fantasy reasoning are also characteristic of this age group. Young children are convinced of the power of their wishes. They believe that they can will a person back to life. Conversely, they think that their thoughts, words, or actions can cause death to occur. If, for example, a child has wished that that a new baby sister would go away, and then the baby dies from SIDS, the child may feel responsible. Or if a parent yells at a child in a moment of exasperation, "You'll be the death of me yet!"

and then the parent dies, the child may feel she has caused it to happen.

Preschoolers may also view actions, rather than the consequences of actions, as being responsible for a death. They believe, for example, that if a person runs into the street and is killed by a car, the death resulted from careless action rather than from the damage done to the body. Death might also be considered as punishment for something thought, said, or done.

Children this age may also associate death with darkness, violence, evil, and sleeping. Nightmares and a fear of the dark can be common.

Children Six to Ten Years of Age

By the time a child enters school, many changes in thinking have occurred. These are the years of questioning. Early school-age children gradually come to accept the idea that death is final, inevitable, universal, and personal. By age six or seven, they suspect that their parents will die someday and that the same fate *might* await them. They may accept the fact that a person has died and will not come back, but they do not yet fully grasp that everyone *must* die, themselves included. It's as if they need to find a middle ground, a compromise of sorts—a place that enables them to acknowledge the reality of death in general, while at the same time keeping it at a distance from their own life.

Although children in this age group are better able to test reality, magical thinking persists with the younger school-aged child continuing to overestimate the power of her wishes. Of more significance, however, is the strong tendency to personify death. Children view death as a taker, something bad that will come and get you and stop your life.

Children may associate death with ghosts, witches, monsters, burglars, or bogeymen. Thus, upon hearing of a death, a child will likely ask, "Who killed him?" In a sense, these death personifications protect children in their belief that only those whom the "death man" catches and carries off will die. Whoever can get away will live.

Children this age also have a predominant fear of mutilation or the fear of bodily injury. Death becomes frightening and dangerous because children worry that some type of scary being will come and take them away.

Reacting to this anxiety, boys in particular seek detailed information about death and bodies. Children try to gain a sense of control through their own rational analysis of the situation. They also use fantasy life to confront death. Death is often play-acted in games of war and violence, and playmates discuss the gory details with one another.

At this age, children begin to establish their own sense of moral judgment, contemplating right from wrong at a general level. They may continue to think of death as retribution for something they have thought, said, or done. These children may also begin to try to reason out the meaning of life and death and to consider the possibility of an afterlife.

Children Ten to Twelve Years of Age

Children this age continue to develop an acute sense of what is right and wrong. Many will still consider death as punishment for misdeeds. Although they are making the transition to more adult understandings of the concept of death, remnants of magical thinking and fantasy reasoning may still be evident.

Early adolescents are learning to understand both the biological process of death and the emotional aspects of it. At this point, they are better able to comprehend the facts surrounding death than they are to understand the associated feelings. Unlike younger children, they now have a frame of reference and are intellectually able to handle much of the same information that is given to an adult.

Death at this age can be understood in relation to the laws of nature. In general, early adolescents may recognize that death is not an external power or being that comes upon them. Rather, it is thought to be an internal dysfunction within the body that causes life to end. These children will likely state the cause of death to be such things as an illness, an accident with serious bodily injury, or old age.

Children this age are experimenting with ideas and theories and may think that death is a way of getting rid of people to make room for new ones. Or they may believe that each time there is a death, there is a birth.

Typically, early adolescents have moved beyond wondering what death is. They are now more focused on relationships and may ask questions such as, "What will happen to our family now that Dad died? Who will take care of Mom?" Concerned with practical issues, they may wonder how their financial situation has been influenced and whether it will require a change in their lifestyle.

On the emotional level, fears of suffocation gradually replace mutilation anxiety. Consequently, concern about death includes a fear of being buried alive. Worries about pain and suffering also begin to surface as children think about their own death.

Children in this age group have reached a turning point in their development. Given their increasing ability to think abstractly, they can now consider death in spiritual terms. Death is understood to be irreversible, universal, personal, and real.

Children Twelve to Eighteen Years of Age

Adolescents hold many adult concepts of death and can cope with it in a similar manner. With cognitive skills that are well developed, they intellectually understand that death is inevitable, irreversible, and universal.

As teenagers search for independence and meaning in life, they become focused on their bodies. They want to be attractive and accepted by their peers. They desire to be different than their parents and tend to use their friends as measures of success or failure in such things as family, school, physical and cognitive abilities, and social life.

Teenagers tend to be focused on the here and now, living in the present moment. At the same time, however, they are also beginning to think about the future and what it might look like for them. Their thoughts become philosophical and they may consider "Who am I? What do I want to do with my life?" They may also ponder death and wonder, "If a person grows up to die, then what is the sense of life?"

Death is especially threatening to adolescents because it can destroy life and the body. It represents the ending of a person's beauty, strength, and capabilities. Death also illustrates that life can be interrupted and that goals can be destroyed and never reached.

Adolescents are faced with significant changes, many of which are beyond their control, such as puberty. People seek a certain degree of autonomy in life. When control is lost in one area, a person is likely to compensate by asserting control in another. For teens, thoughts of death or their own mortality may be too threatening or overwhelming. As a means of dealing with this, they may deny or defy death. Examples of the denial of death include such activities as speeding, experimenting with drugs, and engaging in unprotected sex with multiple partners.

2
Teaching Children about Death

*C*hildren can learn to accept death as a natural aspect of life. It is the responsibility of adults to introduce the concept at an early age in an objective and non-threatening manner. Doing this facilitates the development of a healthy understanding of death. At times—perhaps because of their own inability to confront issues related to death—some parents do not attempt to educate their children about death. They leave the instruction to other people: school teachers, faith formation instructors, health care professionals, and child care providers. This is less than ideal, however, because children's exposure to death may not wait until they have been given a proper "death education."

Far too often the concept of death is not introduced until there is a crisis situation, such as the death of a parent or grandparent. At that point, family members are usually emotionally overwhelmed and find it difficult to adequately explain what has happened. In the ideal situation, children will have the opportunity to learn about death within the context of everyday life *before* they are confronted with the loss of a person (or pet) they love.

Children are naturally inquisitive. As they grow and develop, they are constantly exploring their environment in an attempt to discover how everything works and fits together. Just as children wonder about life, they also wonder about death. It is to their advantage to teach them that death is part of life, just as being born, eating, drinking, sleeping, talking, feeling, laughing, and crying are part of life.

In the Home

Take Advantage of Teachable Moments

Moments within our daily lives provide opportunities for educating children about any number of subjects. These are called teachable moments. Learn to watch for moments related to the life cycle, and use them to introduce and discuss the concept of death. The loss of a person or an animal that you and your child are not particularly close to provides an excellent opportunity to explore the topic in a calm manner at a time when you are not emotionally upset. Here you can identify some of the common responses to loss, help children become familiar with them, and learn to cope with them. As children become aware of various grief rituals, use the opportunities to introduce the concept of public grieving.

Nature itself provides a multitude of common, everyday examples that can raise questions that assist us in teaching about death. A child confronted by a dead bird on the sidewalk is likely to ask, "What happened?" and "Why?" If she does not, initiate the conversation yourself, emphasizing that death is a natural occurrence even though it might make us feel sad.

The changing seasons also illustrate the natural cycle of life and death. Each spring we observe the trees beginning to bud and the flowers beginning to bloom. Throughout the summer, everything continues to grow and flourish. In the fall we see the leaves change colors and fall to the ground. After the first frost, flowers shrivel and die. Over time, the dead leaves and flowers decompose, eventually becoming a part of the soil and providing nourishment for the new life that will emerge in the spring.

Children are also exposed to death through the media. This can be a confusing forum for discussing death, particularly for younger children. Pay attention to what your children are watching and clarify any confusing, contradictory messages that might be implied. As mentioned earlier, cartoon characters who appear to have been killed but then spring back to life are one potential source of confusion. But many children's shows and movies deal wisely and effectively with nature's cycles and can provide many teachable moments. (The "circle of life" in *The Lion King* is a prominent example.)

A number of storybooks and fairytales can also aid in the process of death education. (See pages 125-127 for ideas on further reading.) Ideally these books will have been read with the children before a death occurs within the family. Well-chosen books can supplement or reinforce information gleaned from a teachable moment because the children's curiosity about death will already have been aroused.

By taking advantage of teachable moments, we help children prepare for the personal losses they will inevitably experience.

Share Basic Religious, Spiritual, and Cultural Beliefs about Death

When teaching children about death, it is important to share our religious, spiritual, and cultural beliefs concerning it. Your child's faith or life philosophy begins to develop at a young age. Therefore, it is helpful for them to know about your beliefs so they can integrate them accordingly. For example, you may choose to talk about the soul, heaven, and life after death.

In your conversations, address the questions that arise and emphasize what is most consistent with your personal beliefs. Realize that children hear things from a variety of sources and will benefit from clarification regarding how differing information fits together. If you are unsure about something, admit this. Be honest as to what you know based on fact, as well as what you believe based on your faith and philosophy of life.

Be prepared for tough questions, even from younger children. Questions like, "Why did God make death?" and confusion about death's "unfairness" are likely to be heard from children. As always, be ready to admit if you do not have a firm answer, and use the opportunity to hear your child's response to her own question. This gives you a somewhat direct view of what she is thinking and helps you to frame further answers.

Provide Basic Information about the Causes of Death

When telling children about a specific death, discuss its cause. If the person died from an illness, clarify that it was a very serious illness, rather than one children frequently have such as colds, ear infections, or sore throats. If the death was caused by an accident, clarify that the body was injured so badly that it could no longer work properly.

Provide for Positive Separation Experiences

One of the earliest childhood fears is separation from care-givers. Young children are not able to differentiate between a short, temporary absence and a long, possibly permanent one. Any separation can cause them anxiety.

We can alleviate some of this fear by building positive separation experiences into children's lives. Begin with very short time periods and then gradually lengthen the time that you are away. Leave the children in the care of someone they know and trust. Explain in terms they can understand where you are going and when you will be back. You might say, for example, "Grandma has come to take care of you while Mommy goes to a meeting at church. You can play outside for a bit, and then Grandma will give you lunch and put you to bed for a nap. When you wake up, I will be back."

After you return home, spend some time with your child to see how her time apart from you went. Discuss any concerns she might have and talk about ways to ease them in the future. By being consistent and following through on plans, children become familiar with routine separations and their anxiety related to them decreases. This in turn helps prepare children for more significant separations.

In the School

At school, children should be encouraged to ask questions about things they don't know or understand. Most children lack the knowledge and experience of death, so it should be a fair topic to address.

Take Advantage of Teachable Moments

Many of the teachable moments encountered in the home are also available in school. Educators can improvise during these moments, and then supplement them with more formal treatment in the classroom. To take on the challenge of death education, take advantage of the occurrence of death in the environment (animals, seasonal changes) as well as unexpected deaths in the human community (the death of a school staff member or a fellow student).

Integrate the Concept of Death into the Academic Curriculum

Death education can be structured into the formal academic curriculum by including it in existing courses of study, such as science and health. It can also be taught as a separate course. Those who teach courses on death should:

- have some specialized training in the area of death education
- be aware of, and comfortable with, their own issues about mortality
- demonstrate the ability to discuss death openly and honestly without conveying negative messages, whether verbally or nonverbally, consciously or unconsciously

Some schools allow classroom pets, such as gerbils or goldfish. If the pet dies, students have a timely opportunity to plan a burial, and possibly a service of some sort.

In a science course, children can experience nature's cycles firsthand by planting, nurturing, and harvesting a small garden. In a health class, they may learn how the human body works and discuss the benefits of making healthy choices. Children might discuss the benefits of proper nutrition and exercise, and the harmful effects of drugs and alcohol. Students may also differentiate between common, chronic, and acute illnesses, and talk about what happens when the body is seriously injured. Some classes might even visit a local mortuary to learn more about what happens to the body after death.

In the Faith Community

In faith formation classes, children have the opportunity to discuss the cultural, religious, and spiritual aspects of death.

Take Advantage of Teachable Moments

Children tend to be curious in most environments, the church included. Teachable moments are readily available in this setting as well. A child may wonder about the significance of the crucifix, or might hear a prayer request for a person who is very ill. A death or funeral notice in the church bulletin might provoke questions. We can take advantage of these moments to build upon what the children already know about death, which may or may not include the religious and spiritual aspects of it.

Integrate the Concept of Death into Faith Formation Classes

Children can also be instructed about death in their regular faith formation or religious education classes. The Easter season provides excellent opportunities to talk about this through the obvious example of Jesus' death and resurrection. Discussion of the prophets and martyrs provides other openings for death education in the faith community.

Share Faith as Faith, Not Fact

When discussing our religious and spiritual beliefs with children, it is important that we clarify what we know as fact and what we believe based on our faith and life philosophy. The facts of death are actually rather limited. We know that the body ceases to function for any number of reasons, which means that the person is no longer able to breathe, eat, drink, sleep, talk, laugh, feel, touch, move, or do any of the other things that people who are living can do. The body becomes lifeless—like an empty shell—and is buried, cremated, or donated to science. Although we may visit the physical remains of the deceased, the essential life of the person—often called the soul or the spirit—is no longer present.

Christian faith, not medical science, teaches us that after our death, we too will be reunited in heaven with God and all the other faithful people who have died before us. Beyond this basic doctrine, we enter into speculation. We do not know what or where heaven is, but we believe it to be full of light, joy, and peace. We do not know how the soul or spirit gets to heaven, or whether or not the deceased can see and hear us in our day-to-day lives. Children, being children however, want to know these things.

Children tend to think in concrete terms, so they have difficulty imagining abstractions such as the soul and spirit, God and heaven. In making sense of death, children often fill in the blanks created by the information (or lack of information) we provide based on our faith. Heaven, for example, is often imagined as a place in the sky filled with people who are healthy, happy, and doing their favorite activities. When asked how the deceased get there, children may respond, "Well—on a cloud, of course!"

Such images may have originated with pictures in a storybook or cartoon, or from ideas they have heard from their peers. When addressing children's questions, though, it is often best not to contradict their images. We ourselves do not have all the answers, so what is the harm if their picture of heaven varies from ours? Why take away something that a child finds comforting simply because we may imagine it differently? An exception to this might be an image that not only directly conflicts or contradicts our beliefs, but one that may also be particularly disturbing or frightening for the child. (For example, an image of God as a malevolent being who takes people with no apparent regard to the implications for the people left behind, or as a means of retribution.)

Avoid Portraying God as a Taker

When discussing religious and spiritual beliefs with children, consider how your statements might be misinterpreted. If we say, "God has taken your daddy to be with him in heaven," a child might become angry and disillusioned with a God who would "take away" her dad. Rather than telling children that God takes people, we can say that we don't know why tragedies happen, and then gently reassure them that God is waiting with open arms to receive loved ones when they die.

Avoid Saying, "It Was God's Will"

When children hear that it was "God's will" for a person to die, they may become confused, especially if they have been taught that God is a kind and loving being who watches over us like a parent. If parents do not deliberately hurt their children, why would God do such a thing? If they understand God to be aware of the pain felt by the living when a death occurs, they may wonder why God would "will" such a thing to happen. Children may come to believe that God is not such a kind and loving being after all.

Rather than suggesting that death is God's will, we can explain it as a part of the mystery of life. The mystery of life and death challenges us to grow in faith. Although we do not seek out or ask for pain and difficulties, when we encounter them we can choose how we will live with them. These experiences can be a source of empowerment, or they can consume and destroy us. The choice is ours.

Part Two

Grieving with Children

3

How Children Grieve

*G*rief is a process. It is experienced over time and becomes a part of one's life history. Children in particular will grieve and regrieve a death throughout their lives as they grow and develop and perceive the loss from new developmental perspectives.

Before discussing the various affects of grief, it will be helpful to have an understanding of how your child's grieving process differs from yours as an adult. It is important to note that differences do exist, and that the younger the child the more pronounced these differences will be. Barbara D. Rosof, in *The Worst Loss*, suggests five principle ways in which children's grief differs from that of adults. Children are more physical, less verbal, express their anger very directly, need respites, and attune themselves to parents' needs.

Children have a tendency to experience and express intense emotions in physical ways. Engaging aggressively in physical activity can provide them with an outlet for the expression of these feelings. Children may also express their grief through physical symptoms, some of which may be similar to those of the deceased prior to the death.

Even children who are verbally quite competent are likely to experience some degree of difficulty articulating the intense feelings that are a part of their grief process. Your child will look to you for help in finding the words that go with the emotions she is experiencing.

Children also cope with their feelings through play activities. These activities provide children with an outlet for expression, but also enable them to become more comfortable with circumstances and events that were likely unfamiliar to them before the experience of a loved one's death. In unfamiliar situations, children have a tendency to move toward the familiar, such as favorite toys and activities, as a means to help them cope. Just because they engage in these activities after a death does not mean they are not grieving.

Children also have a tendency to act out their anger and may engage in increased verbal fighting or just seem mad for no apparent reason. It is important to acknowledge their feelings when grieving manifests itself in these types of behavior, while also guiding them to find other, more appropriate ways to express their anger.

It is difficult to deal with the intensity of grief for long periods of time. Children—both because of their limited tolerance for emotional pain and their still developing coping skills—have a particular need to take breaks from the often overwhelming and consuming aspects of the grieving process. The fact that your child grieves in spurts—at times obviously aware of the death and the implications for their life and others seemingly oblivious to this—does not mean that she is not grieving.

More often than we realize, and certainly more extensively than we give them credit for, children are aware of and accommodating to the emotional atmosphere in their home. When your child observes you in the depths of your own grief, they may make a judgment as to how much of their feelings you will be able to handle. If they sense—accurately or not—that you are unable to handle their emotions, they will attempt to protect you by limiting the feelings they share with you. It is important to periodically touch base with your child regarding how she is doing. This will minimize the chance that your child will hide her grief from you for long periods because she has the impression that you cannot bear it.

As a means of understanding your child's grief, it is helpful to be aware of how it may affect her physically, mentally, emotionally, and spiritually. Although your child's grieving will be an individual process influenced by a number of different factors, you will likely note that she will exhibit many of the reactions described in this chapter. Some will occur soon after the death, others may be delayed. In helping your child, it is imperative that you attempt to understand and accept your child's grief response as unique, taking care not to pass judgment or to compare or contrast her reaction with that of another child.

Physical Symptoms

Linda Goldman, in her book *Life and Loss,* lists physical symptoms some grieving children experience: fatigue, headaches, shortness of breath, dry mouth, dizziness, pounding heart, hot or cold flashes, heaviness of body, sensitive skin, an empty feeling in the body, tightness in the chest and throat, muscle weakness, stomach aches, and increased illness. Children who are grieving may also report physical symptoms similar to those of the deceased prior to death.

The cause of these symptoms can be multifaceted, and it will be important to explore them with your child so you are able to deal with them appropriately.

Grieving children's physical symptoms may be indicated in statements like these:

- I'm tired but I can't sleep.
- I don't feel good. My head hurts.
- I'm not hungry. My stomach hurts.
- I feel sick like Billy did. Maybe I'm going to die, too?

Children may express bodily distress because they are confused about what causes death, and they may be frightened that they, too, might die. If this is the case, ask your child what they know and think about death. Clarify misconceptions in understandable language. If the death resulted from an illness, explain the difference between common, chronic, and acute illnesses. If an accident was involved, let them know that it was a very serious one and that the person's body was hurt so badly that it could no longer work right. With both illnesses and accidents, tell your child about the ways you take care of both yourself and her in order to remain as healthy and safe as possible.

Physical symptoms can also be your child's way of seeking additional attention. Reassure her that although this is a difficult time for everyone, you love her very much and will do your best to continue to give her the attention she needs.

Thought Patterns

Linda Goldman also describes the thought patterns often seen in grieving children. They have an inability to concentrate and difficulty making decisions. They sometimes have self-destructive thoughts and a low self-image, and show signs of preoccupation, confusion, and disbelief. It may sometimes seem as if your child is in her own little world and not paying attention. The following statements demonstrate these thought patterns:

- I can't concentrate.
- I just don't know what to do.
- How can I live without her? Maybe I'd be better off dead with her.
- I remember how we used to . . .
- How did this happen? Why did this happen? It doesn't make sense.
- I can't believe it. I know she didn't die!

Bereaved children—like adults—may have difficulty paying attention or concentrating for any length of time. Explain that this is normal, and that in time it will be easier to focus. Reassure the child that you are aware that it might be hard to concentrate on her schoolwork and let her know you do not expect her to do as well right now. Be sure to tell the child's teachers of the death. This will enable them to be prepared for any possible behavior changes.

Grieving children may find themselves thinking about the deceased all the time. It's as if there is no escape from the memories, as there are constant reminders wherever they look. These reminders may cause the children to experience unrelenting pain. In an attempt to find some relief from the overwhelming sadness, they may withdraw from the people and things that remind them of the deceased. Assure the child that this is normal, that you are all remembering the person who has died. Share your memories and talk about your feelings. Let your child know that you want to help her, and emphasize that running away from the situation will not make it go away.

Emotional Responses

Linda Goldman identifies the emotions experienced by grieving children. They feel unreal, angry, guilty, sad. They have mood swings and feelings of depression, hysteria, relief, helplessness, fear, loneliness, anxiety, and rage. Their feelings can be intense. These emotions are made evident in the following statements:

- It's like a bad dream, and I just want to wake up.
- How could Mommy die and leave me?
- Why didn't the doctor save him?
- Why did God let this happen?
- If only I hadn't yelled at him, he'd still be alive.
- I shouldn't have said I hated her.
- I miss him all the time.
- Are you going to die too, Daddy?
- Who will take care of me?
- I hate him for dying!
- I start crying and I don't know why.

It is common for children to deny that a death has occurred. Denial is a part of the grieving process. Death often comes as a surprise, and children react in shock. Information that is painful and difficult may be pushed aside or denied for a time. Upon hearing of a death, children will often resume play almost immediately. This does not mean that they did not love the deceased or that they are unaffected by the death. Rather, denial provides a period of reprieve from the overwhelming sense of loss that usually accompanies death. Just as adults need to take a break from the intensity of the situation, children do as well.

Bereaved children often feel angry about the death of someone close. Their anger may stem from a feeling of helplessness or a loss of control, and typically it will be directed outwardly. Your child may, for example, be openly angry at the person who died for having left at a time when she needed that person. This feeling can be intensified when they perceive the deceased as having had a choice in their death, as in a suicide. Children may also direct their anger at others, such as God or the doctor, for not having saved their loved one. Children's anger can also be expressed less directly by acting out at school or home. Either way, it is important that you understand and accept this anger for what it is. Reassure your child that it is okay to be mad, and help her find appropriate ways of venting her anger.

At times, children who are grieving may turn their anger inward, blaming themselves for the death. Your child may believe that something she thought, said, or did somehow caused the death to occur. Explore your child's feelings with her. Listen for any misconceptions she might have and help her to clarify them. Review the cause of the death with your child and emphasize that something in the person's body was not working right because of an illness or injury. Reassure her that she is not responsible for the death.

Children tend to be self-oriented. Thus, when a death occurs and the structure of their lives change, it is not uncommon for them to worry about how their needs will be met. This is especially true when the deceased is a parent (these children will frequently be heard asking the surviving parent, "Who will take care of me when you die?"). Your child needs to know that you love her very much and that she will always be taken care of. Talk with her about all the people who love her and identify who would be responsible for her in the unfortunate event that you were to die. Emphasize that you hope to live for a long time.

Common Behavior Changes

Emotional responses and thought patterns influence the behaviors seen in children who are grieving. Goldman identifies sleeplessness, loss of appetite, poor grades, crying, nightmares, dreams about the deceased, sighing, listlessness, absent-mindedness, over-activity, social withdrawal, verbal attacks, fighting, extreme quietness, bed-wetting, clinging, excessive touching, and excessive hugging as behaviors often seen in grieving children. They are evident in the following statements and observations by and about grieving children.

- She can't seem to sleep well anymore. She often wakes up crying.
- He's just not hungry anymore.
- I have this dream about my dad.
- She used to be a pretty good student.
- I can't remember what I'm supposed to be doing.
- He can't seem to sit still. He starts doing one thing and then moves right on to something else.
- She doesn't do much with her friends anymore.
- It's like he goes out of his way to pick a fight or get in trouble.
- She hasn't wet the bed in a long time, and now she is again.
- Please don't leave me, Mommy. I don't want you to go.
- Grandpa, do you love me as much as my daddy did?
- I can bake cookies just like my grandma did.
- Don't I look like my mom?
- My daddy was the best in the whole world!

Grieving children may become overactive, searching aimlessly for something to do and jumping from one activity to another without an obvious purpose. They may also talk or giggle incessantly as they attempt to cope with the death.

Bereaved children may withdraw from the people they love, afraid that they, too, might die. They may also avoid getting to know new people because they are concerned about being hurt again. Acknowledge that although there is always the possibility that someone we love may die sooner than expected, being able to know and love the person makes it worth the risk. Communicate your love for your child, and try to help her see that by withdrawing from other people, she is cutting herself off from support at a time when she needs it most.

The death of a loved one often causes significant changes in a child's routine. The security of their daily life has been disrupted, and they may be overwhelmed. Lacking an adult's ability to cope, they may regress to earlier behaviors such as bed-wetting, imaginary friends, and increased independence on adults. In light of this, it will be important for you to try to follow your child's normal routine as closely as possible and help to restore a sense of order and security. You will also want to avoid making any unnecessary changes that could increase your child's stress and further disrupt her life.

Many children will become tearful and clingy when they anticipate a separation. Now that they have experienced a death—and have some understanding of the implications of it for their lives—they have a concern that other loved ones might also die. Acknowledge your child's anxiety and try to reduce it by preparing her for those times when you will be separated. Explain where you are going, whom you will be with, what you will be doing, and when you will be back in terms she will understand.

Bereaved children may also try to replace the deceased by seeking the attention of another person. Tell your child that everyone will miss the person who has died and that it will be difficult to live without him or her. Reassure your child that although no one can ever take the place of the deceased, there will always be other people to know and love.

At times children may assume certain mannerisms of the deceased and begin acting or talking like that person. Remind your child that you love her for who she is. Emphasize that although she may have some of the characteristics of the deceased, she is special and unique in her own right.

Children who are grieving may also remember only the good things about the person who has died. While it is comforting to remember these points, it is not healthy for your child to fantasize that the deceased was perfect or to deny any memories that contradict this. If you allow your child to idealize the person who has died, she may develop unrealistic expectations of other people and herself. Emphasize that no one—not even the deceased—is perfect, but that does not prevent us from loving one another.

Spiritual Responses

When considering how your child experiences grief spiritually, It is important to draw a distinction between religion and spirituality. Religion is the organized or formal expression of shared beliefs with a faith community. Spirituality is comprised of one's deepest personal beliefs. It provides meaning and a connection to a higher power of some kind. When people experience the death of a significant person, it is not uncommon for them to find themselves in a period of profound questioning—a time in which they may struggle deeply with previously held beliefs.

Children tend to experience their spiritual questioning as a disruption in their sense of security, stability, predictability, and fairness in life. Their world has been turned upside down, leaving them wondering what to expect and who or what to depend upon. They have experienced that bad things can in fact happen and that life isn't always fair. Grieving children—and adults as well—will ideally be able to draw some meaning from the death and integrate that meaning into their lives. In this process, their original beliefs will either be affirmed and strengthened or adjusted in some way.

In closing, it is important to note that in some cases bereaved children may be unable to grieve the loss when it happens. This could be caused by a number of factors, such as their age or the support that is available to them at the time of the death. Whatever the reason, if children do not deal effectively with feelings related to the death, they will not simply go away with time. At some point in the future, something will trigger these emotions and they will be confronted with the grief that had been repressed earlier.

4

Understanding Grief
and Its Tasks

*G*rief can be defined as a normal, internalized reaction to a loss. Part of the reaction involves adaptation to the loss. In this chapter, we will look at the process of grief and the tasks associated with it.

Grieving is extremely painful; at the same time, it is absolutely essential that we do it. Grief will not simply go away with the passage of time or a determined effort to ignore or avoid it. When someone we love dies, it is as if our lives stop. We become immobilized by our loss. If we don't grieve—for whatever reason—our lives remain stuck. The work of coming to terms with the reality that our loved one has died is ultimately what enables us to move ahead, however altered life might now be.

Some grief educators have proposed that because grief is a process, it should be viewed as having stages or phases. Others have associated tasks with grieving, suggesting that these tasks not only comprise the work of grief, but also offer a means of understanding it. However you choose to look at grief, it is critical that you consider its ongoing nature.

Many people are familiar with the pioneering work of Dr. Elisabeth Kübler-Ross and her book *On Death and Dying*. Working with people who were dying, Kübler-Ross identified stages these patients experienced as they approached death: denial, anger, bargaining, depression, and acceptance. Readers often understood these stages quite literally and assumed, therefore, that people who were dying would pass through them in a sequential, orderly fashion. It is my impression, however, that Kübler-Ross understood that dying is a variable process and that its stages should not be viewed as rigid or linear.

It is important to remember that Kübler-Ross developed her stages in reference to the experience of dying. They have also been widely applied to the experience of grieving. When applied to grieving, though, the misinterpretation that the stages are sequential and orderly conflicts with the understanding that grief is a process, and that people move through its stages in varying order and may experience particular stages more than once or not at all.

We will return to Kübler-Ross's stages of dying later, when we discuss the issue of dying children. Now we will look at the stages of grieving and the tasks that those in grief must work to accomplish throughout the process.

The Stages and Tasks of Grieving

A general listing of the stages of grief includes the following: shock and disbelief, searching and yearning, disorganization and despair, and rebuilding and healing.

Upon learning of a death, we experience a period of shock and numbness. This stage enables us to disregard the fact of the loss for a brief time; it provides a buffer between us and something that seems unbearable. The next stage, searching and yearning, involves searching both for the deceased and for the meaning of their death, as well as yearning for their return. In the third stage, disorganization and despair, the grieving person experiences difficulty functioning in the environment. The fourth stage, rebuilding and healing, finds us gradually beginning to pull the pieces of our lives back into an orderly condition.

It is important to note that movement through the stages does not occur in a neat and orderly manner. There may be overlaps, and people may experience some of the stages more than once. At times this can be very confusing, and people may wonder if they are going "crazy." Be assured that this is all a part of the process.

Sandra Fox, in *Good Grief: Helping Groups of Children When a Friend Dies*, states that for grieving children to make their grief "good" they must accomplish three tasks: understanding, grieving, and commemorating. J. William Worden, author of *Grief Counseling and Grief Therapy*, proposes four tasks: accepting the reality of the loss, working through the pain of grief, adjusting to an environment in which the deceased is missing, and emotionally "relocating" the deceased and moving on with life.

In considering the grief experience, I have found the tasks of both Fox and Worden to be helpful. Not only do these tasks define the "grief work" that Worden believes must be completed for healing to occur, they also provide a means for understanding grief. Their tasks present a number of paral-lels, as shown in the table below, and will be discussed in connection with one another.

Fox	Worden
1. Understanding	1. Accepting the reality of the loss
2. Grieving	2. Working together through the pain of grief
3. Commemorating	3. Adjusting to an environment in which the deceased is missing
	4. Emotionally "relocating" the deceased and moving on with life

Understanding and Accepting

For children, understanding the death requires that they know the person is dead, that he or she is gone and will never again return to the child's daily life. To achieve this task, children need honest information that is shared in terms they can understand.

Initially, you'll want to inform your child of the death with a simple explanation. Be careful not to overwhelm her with information or details she is not yet ready for. Tell her the basic facts of the death itself, and include a clear descrip-tion of what the word *dead* means. Let her know that you will answer any questions she might have and provide her with an opportunity to express any and all of her feelings.

Your child will likely think about this initial explanation and then seek out additional details as she is ready for them. Answer the questions she asks. Provide honest information. You can build upon this foundation of truth over time.

Accepting the reality of the loss takes time. This involves both intellectual and emotional acceptance.

Although a person may be cognitively aware of the finality of the death, it may take longer to achieve full emotional acceptance. Participation in traditional rituals, such as the funeral, can help achieve the task of acceptance.

Grieving and Working through the Pain

Grieving involves working through many and various feelings. Although adults and children grieve in similar and predictable ways, it is imperative to recognize that, despite the similarities, the experience is unique for each individual. Just as the relationship between the deceased and the bereaved was unique, so, too, is the sense of loss.

Whenever someone we love dies, we will experience pain. Although the intensity and expression of this pain may vary, the fact of its presence does not. It is therefore necessary to work through this pain in order to grieve effectively. If the pain is avoided, if we refuse to feel the feelings, it will not simply go away. It will remain until it has been addressed properly.

Various formal rituals (the viewing or wake, the funeral, the burial, or the memorial service) can help children channel their grief appropriately. When planning for these, it will be important to take children's needs into account. These observances tend to be geared to an adult expression of grief. Children are often forgotten or overlooked.

Participation in these rituals can facilitate the accomplishment of both tasks one and two as proposed by Fox and Worden. Not only can it move children toward an acceptance of the death, but participation will also assist them in working through the emotional aspects of it. I am a strong advocate for involving children of all ages in some level of the planning of, and participation in, these rituals. This places children in the position of facing the reality of the death, and provides them with opportunities for actively grieving it.

Children usually want to be included in the family's grieving. They choose, more often than not, to be active participants if they are engaged in a manner that is honest, encouraging, and supportive.

Although adults often make the final decisions about children's participation in these events, even very young children can be encouraged to talk about what is happening and what they want to do. Tell your child about the funeral and other services and events. Explain the rituals in language they can understand, stating that these provide us with ways to say goodbye and show our respect to the person who has died. When given a clear description of what will happen, as well as a choice about their own participation, children typically let us know what they want to do.

Ideally, each child will be encouraged to participate at whatever level she feels comfortable. Children should not feel pressured into doing something that isn't comfortable just because others are doing it. Support your child and provide her with options. Some children will want to be actively involved in all of the formal rituals, while others will choose to attend only some of them. Some children may choose to view and touch the body, while others will avoid such contact.

You may choose to schedule a private viewing for children only. This will ensure that they can, if they want, see and touch the body in the presence of people they love and trust, without the distracting presence of extended family members and friends. The funeral director can be available during this time to answer questions and concerns raised by the children. This enables you to understand what your child is thinking, but also takes pressure off you at a time when you may be overwhelmed by your own grief and unable to respond adequately to her questions.

At the funeral, it may be helpful to have an understanding adult on hand who can be available to your child. This person's role is to respond to your child's needs, answer her questions, provide support, and take her outside if she becomes restless or disruptive. This allows you to participate in the service without having to take full responsibility for the care of your child.

If your child chooses not to attend the funeral, consider having it videotaped for future reference. There will undoubtedly be a time when she will want to know more about the service, and having the tape will provide her with the opportunity.

Commemorating, Adjusting, "Relocating"

Formal and Informal Commemoration

We commemorate in order to honor or keep alive the memory of someone or something. Commemoration provides us with a way to remember that which has been lost, and can take place in a formal or informal manner. Grieving children should be invited to participate, in appropriate ways, in both manners of commemoration.

Formal commemoration includes memorial services, tributes in a yearbook or newsletter, commemorative plaques, donations to a specific charity, or the establishment of a scholarship fund. Informal commemoration often involves doing something tangible as a means of remembering the deceased. Share your favorite memories of the person with your child and invite her to do the same with you. If possible, offer your child a possession from the deceased that holds a special meaning. This could be a special CD from an older sibling, a fishing pole from a grandfather, or a favorite piece of jewelry from a mother.

Ask your child how she wants to remember her loved one, and then help her to find ways to do this. If, for example, Johnny and his grandpa spent a lot of time fishing together, maybe on the anniversary of the death you and your child could go back to a favorite fishing spot. Or, if

Emily and her grandmother used to enjoy picnics under a tree in grandma's backyard, maybe Emily would like to plant a similar tree in her own yard. Assisting children with such memorials facilitates healthy resolution of grief. Whatever the method of commemoration, it should be sensitive to the wishes and needs of the deceased person's family and friends and be helpful in facilitating the grief process. Eventually, acts of formal or informal commemoration—so important at the time of the death—become less needed as grievers adjust to the loss.

Adjusting to an Environment in Which the Deceased Is Missing

Worden states that adjusting to an environment without the deceased means different things to different people. Making the adjustment depends on your child's relationship with the deceased and the various roles the deceased played in her life. It is not unusual for it to take significant time after the loss for the bereaved person to adjust to living without the person who has died.

The bereaved person may be faced with a number of adjustments. She may need to adjust to the loss of roles formerly played by the deceased, such as in the case of a surviving wife who depended on her husband for most of the driving. The survivor may also need to adjust his or her own sense of self, as in the case of a parent whose child has died and has thus lost a clear sense of being Mom or Dad. He or she may need to adjust to a new sense of the world, in which new questions brought on by the death challenge previous assumptions and beliefs.

Grievers find it necessary to learn new roles, develop new skills, and face life with new ways of understanding. Adjustment is a complex process, no less for children and young people as for adults, as the following story shows:

Karla was fourteen years old when her father died suddenly. Karla and her father were very close. He used to help her with her homework and attended her track meets and basketball games. Her dad was a deeply spiritual man and taught faith formation classes at their church.

When he died, Karla's life changed significantly. Her mom had always been at home, but now had to take a job. This meant that Karla had to help more around the house. She and her younger brother, George, frequently came home to an empty house and were responsible for doing their homework and starting dinner. Karla continued to run track and play basketball, but it didn't seem as much fun as it had before. Her faith was severely challenged, and she struggled to make sense of a God who would allow her father to die when she needed him the most.

As time passed, Karla learned to enjoy cooking and started to feel good about being able to help her mother with housekeeping. She realized that running was something she could do with her brother, and convinced him to join the high school team. Karla sought guidance from their parish priest, desperately wanting to believe again in a loving God.

Gradually, Karla came to accept that all people die. Although she may never understand why her father died when he did, Karla found comfort in the belief that God shares her grief. Rather than thinking of God as having taken her father, Karla now imagines God as having been there to welcome her dad to heaven when his life on earth was complete. She misses her dad's daily presence in her life, but finds comfort in knowing that he is with her in her heart. As a tribute to him, she eventually became a Sunday school teacher, sharing her faith and instructing children as her dad had done.

When a person dies, we are faced with the task of finding an appropriate place for the dead in our emotional lives. The thoughts and memories associated with the deceased will never be lost. Over time, however, they must be relocated in our emotional life if we are to move forward. Holding on to the past attachment or relationship can prevent us from going on and developing new ones. The fact that one moves on and establishes new relationships does not in any way minimize the love for the deceased. It signals, rather, that there are other people to love and that we are engaged in the task of moving on with life. This delicate task is illustrated by the following example:

Peter was five years old when his little brother, John, died in a drowning accident. John had been just one year younger than Peter, and they had been the best of friends. They spent hours playing together, and it was difficult for both when Peter started kindergarten. John used to wait on the front steps each afternoon, eagerly waiting for the school bus that would bring his brother—his playmate—home.

On the day of the accident, they had been swimming at the community pool. Typically they were always together, but on this day they became separated while waiting in line for the slide. Somehow John had bumped his head and gone under water without being noticed. Peter witnessed the attempts to resuscitate his brother and was devastated when his mom gently told him that John had died. Peter couldn't believe that John was dead. He barely looked at John's body in the casket and refused to go to the burial. Each day when he got off the bus he looked for John.

Peter gradually began to accept that John really wasn't coming back, just as his mom had said he wasn't. He spent hours sitting in the room he had shared with his brother.

Peter thought of all the fun things they had done together, and became angry when he realized that he and John would never play together again. His mother tried to get him to do things with some of his friends from school, but Peter wasn't interested. They weren't John. They didn't play like John; they weren't fun like John.

Meanwhile, a new family moved into the house next door. Peter's mom told him that there were two girls and one boy. The boy, Tim, was five—just a little bit older than John would have been. At first, Peter didn't want anything to do with Tim. It was too painful. If anything, it should have been he and John together that got to know Tim. But John wasn't here.

Peter's mom began to ask Tim to come over for lunch on Saturdays. Slowly, Peter began to enjoy Tim's company. They started to play together after school, just as he and John had done. At first, Peter felt rather strange about this. He wondered if it was okay to have fun again. Did it mean he didn't miss John? Or maybe that he hadn't loved him enough?

Fortunately, Peter was able to talk with his mother about almost everything, and one day she asked him about how it felt to have a new friend. Peter confided that he felt sort of mixed up about it. He really liked Tim and they had a lot of fun together. Peter still missed his brother, but he was discovering that he could be happy again. He asked his mom if this was okay, or did it mean he didn't love John. His mom assured him that John would always be his brother; that he would always be with them in their hearts. She said they had all loved John very much and that they would never forget him.

Peter and his mom had talked openly about John after his death, sharing their memories and thinking about what he would be doing if he were there with them. His mom suggested that maybe it might be helpful to talk with Tim about his brother, to share some of his favorite stories about him.

Peter began to do this and found that it was helpful to remember John in this way.

Living with the Death during a Lifetime

The grieving process has been likened to the waves of the ocean. The natural feelings of grief are often experienced as an ebb and flow. We can choose to prepare ourselves to ride with the flow, or we can resist its driving force. In making this choice, it is important to remember that grief will not simply go away because time passes or we choose to ignore it. Even if buried deep within our self, the feelings of grief will one day rise again to the surface and demand our attention.

As people grieve the loss of a loved one and search for the meaning it has for their lives, they will find that there are times when grief is all-consuming. This is almost certain to be the case in the days immediately following the death. Through participating in some of the traditional rituals surrounding the death, the feeling of all-consuming grief begins to diminish. Although some may continue to think of the deceased for much of the day, there will be brief moments when grief is not the main focus. Inevitably, however, memories and emotions will come flooding back, leaving the bereaved to wonder if life will ever again contain a sense of calm.

In the months following the death, those who are grieving will continue to experience their grief in waves. As you and your child return to routine activities or patterns of living, you may take a measure of comfort in the security that these provide. Although the grief remains, ideally it will become a part—rather than all—of you. In this process, it will be important for you and your child to face the feelings that the death has brought forth. Be open in your discussions with your child and freely share the special memories that you have of your loved one.

When considering the question of whether or not there is an end to grieving, it is important to know that there is no easy or definitive answer. Bereavement literature attempts to provide some guidelines regarding a timeframe, but in a process as individualized as grieving, there is no conclusive schedule. There seems to be a growing consensus, however, that it can take at least one year, if not two, to fully grieve the death of someone important to you. The year immediately following the death will contain a number of significant "firsts"—the first birthday of the deceased since his or her death; your birthday and your child's birthday; Christmas or Hanukkah; the anniversary of the death. It is important to plan for these days. Take time to consider what you want to do and with whom you want to spend them. Do what you determine to be best for you and your child.

Children will grieve and re-grieve the death throughout the course of their lifetime. Normal developmental milestones in a child's life typically trigger the recurrence of grief. Such milestones—the first day of school, graduation, getting married, becoming a parent—are significant for your child in any case. A child with grief issues may need extra support when these milestones occur.

Your journey of grief with your child is a lifelong process. Although you will undoubtedly encounter people who want you to "get over" your grief, you have likely realized that this is not the goal you are moving toward. Ultimately you and your child will learn to live with the loss and its implications for your lives. You will come to embrace the meaning of the death, weaving it carefully into the fabric of your lives. The person who died was a part of your lives, and your memories of him or her remain with you. Early in the grieving process this may seem overwhelming, perhaps even inconceivable. You have been devastated; it is difficult to imagine life beyond the pain and intensity of the current moment. You will find, however, that the time will come when your sadness has lightened and memories of the deceased bring with them a gentle comfort. The waves of emotion—although continuing now and again to wash over you—do so less often and with decreased intensity. Life will one day hold new hopes and dreams for you and your child, and you will know again the joy that hopes and dreams can bring forth.

5

Helping Children Grieve

As adults—and as parents, even more so—we want to protect children from emotional and physical pain. It is not uncommon to hear someone say, "If only I could make it better for her" or "I would give anything to trade places with her or to have had this not even happen in the first place." Life happens—and in it there is the potential for both great joy and devastating sadness. While we cannot change the fact that a death has occurred, we can have a significant impact on a child's experience of it. Rather than remain passive and lament about that which is beyond our control, it is helpful instead to focus on what we can do.

Talking to Children about a Death

Children are naturally inquisitive about all aspects of life—and the cycle inherent within life—and will seek information in their attempts to gain an understanding of it. Ideally, they will have a general knowledge of the concept of death before being faced with it on a very personal level. In any case, you will need to ensure that discussions with your child include information about the basic facts of death, as these will provide the foundation you will build upon.

Prior to talking with your child about a specific death that has occurred, it will be important for you to give some thought to how you feel about death in general, as well as your own mortality. You will also want to reflect on the circumstances surrounding the recent death and the meaning that it will have for you and your child.

Remember that, as mentioned earlier, children are astute and can often "read" our nonverbal communication. If we are uncomfortable when we talk about death, we may unknowingly convey a message that death is something to be feared or dreaded. Although our words may be saying one thing, nonverbally we may be sending a contradictory or conflicting message through our tone of voice, our eyes, or our posture.

When a death occurs, your child will have a number of questions that need to be explored and answered. These can range from questions that address the cause of the death and the context in which it occurred to those that deal with the matter of what will happen to the body. Children may consider what impact the death will have on their lives, both now and in the future. They may also wonder what the death might mean for other people. Children can have concerns about their own vulnerability and become anxious that they, too, will die. They may also mistakenly believe that they are in some way responsible for the death. Certainly, we will be in a much better position to respond to these questions and concerns in a helpful manner if we have pondered them beforehand during our own reflections.

Informing Your Child about the Death

Every situation involving death is different. Before discussing the death with your child, consider the following:

- What is the age and maturity level of your child?
- What is your child's understanding of the meaning of the words "died" and "dead?"
- Has your child experienced a death prior to this one (perhaps a family pet, a grandparent or parent, a friend, a teacher, or classmate?)
- What is the relationship of your child with the deceased? How well did they know each other and how did they get along?
- What are the circumstances surrounding the death?
- What is your child's typical pattern of coping with difficult situations?
- What are your family's religious, spiritual, and cultural beliefs about death?

The answers to these questions provide general information about your child's understanding of, and experience with, death. As discussed in the first chapter, children gradually develop a concept of death that is directly related to their age, but which is influenced by numerous other factors as well. The older or more mature child will have a more comprehensive understanding of death, as will the child who has previously been touched by it. In a situation in which the child and the deceased were emotionally close, the feelings of grief will be more intense than if they were not significantly attached.

The nature of the death will have an influence on how your child deals with it. A death following a lingering illness is different than one that is sudden or related to suicide or a traumatic incident. A death that was relatively peaceful is in sharp contrast to one that involves violence. If a grandparent has died after a prolonged illness, your child will likely have an awareness of the decline in health that preceded the death. To some extent this may have enabled her to anticipate the outcome and to begin to prepare for it and even to say a direct goodbye. A sudden, unexpected death typically does not allow for this. This is not to say that one situation is easier to deal with than another. Rather, it illustrates that the circumstances surrounding death are variable and it is important to understand what these differences can mean in regard to your child's grieving process.

The child's usual patterns of coping also influence how she deals with the death. If your child faces life head-on—comfortable in seeking the information and support she needs from you—it is likely she will approach the matter of death in the same way. If, however, she typically copes with difficult situations by denying or resisting them, you can probably expect a similar response now.

Your family's religious, spiritual, and cultural views also need to be considered. The child whose family believes in life after death might be comforted by the thought of Grandma and Grandpa being reunited in heaven with God. The culture that embraces aging and death as a natural progression on one's journey may instill or promote a greater sense of understanding or acceptance of the death.

Open the Lines of Communication

When you are prepared to tell your child about the death, find a quiet, comfortable place that will allow you and your child to talk freely and without interruption. During this initial conversation, provide only the basic information. State simply who has died and what the general circumstances were. Avoid overloading your child with too many details.

She will probably be overwhelmed and unable to take in the specifics at this time. The goal is to open the lines for further communication so that your child will feel comfortable asking for additional information later.

It is important that your child have information regarding the death relatively soon after it has occurred. If time or other circumstances prohibit you from being able to do this, consider having someone who has a significant relationship with your child do this for you.

Also, if at any time you cannot deal with your child's questions (for example, when you are physically or emotionally exhausted), tell her why you can't explain now. Tell her that you will discuss her questions and concerns with her as soon as you can. If you fail to do this, your child might think you are avoiding issues or withholding information. This in turn may cause her to question both your integrity and your willingness to talk with her.

Answer Truthfully

All children understand the experience of death at some level, so their questions regarding it must be answered truthfully and in words they can understand. Children seek a beginning, middle, and end to a story. If they sense that information is missing, they will fill in the gaps on their own. Often their imaginative answers turn out to be far more disturbing than the truth itself. Children can be spared the terror of their imaginations if they are given truthful information in a simple, direct manner, as can be seen in the following example:

When Kathy, a seven-year-old, was told that her grandfather had been killed in a car accident, she was worried about what had happened to his body. Although Kathy knew her grandpa was dead, the thought of him being disfigured was really unsettling. She asked her parents about the accident and the injuries that her grandfather had sustained, but they wouldn't talk about it because they worried it might be too frightening. When Kathy was finally able to view the body at the wake, however, she was relieved to see that her grandpa—although cut and bruised—didn't look nearly as bad as she had feared.

By the same token, providing answers that are inconsistent can be confusing for your child and cause her to become anxious and unsettled. She may also determine intuitively that she cannot trust you or rely upon you for information during her grief process.

Answer Only What Is Being Asked

When answering your child's questions, be sure you understand what she is asking and provide only the information she needs at this time. Referring your child's questions back to her can clarify her specific concerns and inform you regarding what is bothering her. Children often have an idea of the answer to their question in their heads, and they are seeking clarification regarding it. The following example illustrates the importance of understanding the question in order that you respond appropriately:

Peggy's big brother, Tom, died recently, and she has just asked you what will happen to his body now. You respond by asking, "What do you think, Peggy?" If she tells you something about Tom going to heaven where he will be able to play baseball all day, then you will have an idea of what she is thinking. You can respond appropriately, exploring her concept of heaven and sharing memories of Tom playing baseball. Imagine how Peggy would have felt if you hadn't asked what she was thinking and had gone instead into a detailed explanation about how the body is embalmed and then buried!

Encourage the Expression of Feelings

Convey to your child that it is all right to show her emotions. Let her know that whatever feelings she has are okay and that everyone expresses their emotions—even similar ones—in different ways.

Children look to their parents for guidance and will often model their behavior after them. If you openly share your feelings with your child, this will encourage her to do the same. It will also minimize the potential for miscommunication or misinterpretation that can result from keeping your feelings hidden. The importance of sharing your feelings with your child is evident in the following example:

Jeff's mom has recently died following a short illness. Fortunately his dad talks openly with him about how much he misses Jeff's mom and how sad he feels now that she is not here with them. Jeff, in turn, talks about his sadness as well. On the other hand, if Jeff rarely hears his dad talk about his feelings and he if never sees his tears, Jeff might get the message that it's not okay to cry. He may even wonder if his dad loved his mom or if he misses her. Although Jeff's dad may cry in the shower and in bed at night, if this expression of emotion is completely hidden from Jeff, it leaves him questioning his dad and wondering what to do with his own emotions.

What is critical in this is not only that we have the feelings, but what we *do* with those feelings. If we demonstrate an ability to cope with feelings effectively, this conveys a sense of comfort or security to the child. On the other hand, it can be very frightening to a child if we become disabled by our feelings and unable to function. Given their dependence on us, children need to know that they will be taken care of even in the face of grief.

Help your child realize that although everyone has similar feelings, each person expresses them differently. By sharing your emotions openly and honestly, your child will be much more likely to feel comfortable expressing her own. Fewer problems develop when children don't have to guess how others are feeling and grieving.

Accept the Child's Feelings and Reactions

Avoid telling children how they should or should not feel and how they should or should not act. Although there are many common feelings and reactions to death, the grieving process for each child will be somewhat different. It is imperative that we recognize and respect this. Children in the same family can respond to the death of their parent differently, as illustrated in the following example:

Matt and McKayla's mother has died following a long illness. Five-year-old Matt appears to be quite angry, whereas ten-year-old McKayla talks freely about her sadness. When discussing this with the children, Matt tells you that he is mad at his mom for dying and leaving him. Not long before she died, Matt overheard his mother saying to his dad that she was at peace and prepared to die. Matt interpreted this to mean that his mother had chosen to die, which also meant leaving him behind. He is feeling abandoned and wonders who will take care of him now that she is gone. McKayla, on the other hand, is old enough to understand that her mother was very ill and there was nothing more that could be done to make her better. Although McKayla is relieved that her mother will no longer be in pain, it is overwhelming to think of life without her loving presence and guidance. Both of these children's feelings are valid and need to be accepted and understood for what they are.

It is also important to note that children's grief comes in waves. It is not uncommon to experience them grieving in bursts—crying one moment and then busily playing the next. This doesn't mean they didn't love the deceased. Rather, it is a function of how children grieve.

Avoid Euphemisms and Untruthful Explanations

When talking with your child about death, avoid using euphemisms. With euphemisms, we use indirect words or phrases in reference to topics we are uncomfortable with addressing directly. It is common to hear the following expressions used to describe someone who has died: gone away, eternal rest, sleeping, passed on, lost, left us, and gone on a trip. Direct expressions like dead, died, or stopped breathing convey the fact that the body is no longer physically alive.

As adults, we can put euphemisms into context and decipher their meaning. Children often cannot. Whereas we may find comfort in the words, for children they can be quite confusing given the more typical meanings they have in daily life.

Sam is three years old and his mother has just told him, "We lost your grandma today." In Sam's mind this isn't a big deal. He remembers getting lost at the grocery store and being found by his dad. All they have to do is go look for grandma and find her, and then everything will be okay.

Mary is seven and has been told that her father was "taken in his sleep." She is not, however, informed that her dad had a heart attack during the night. Mary becomes quite frightened and resists going to bed at night, fearing that she too could be "taken."

Explanations that simply avoid the truth of the situation also shouldn't be used. When a significant person in a child's life "disappears" because he or she has died, any explanation short of the truth is likely to cause confusion and hurt, if not right away then perhaps in the future.

Jessica's favorite uncle has died unexpectedly. Her parents—wanting to protect her from the pain this news will cause—tell her that he has gone away on a long trip and won't be able to visit anymore. Jessica is confused and hurt.

Her uncle is very special to her, and Jessica is confused about why he would choose to go away and not come back. Jessica wonders if maybe she said something that made him not like her anymore.

Integrate Religious, Spiritual, and Cultural Beliefs

When discussing death with your child, be careful to share only information that is consistent with your religious, spiritual, and cultural beliefs regarding the soul, heaven, and life after death. Realize that what may be comforting to you as an adult can be confusing and even frightening to your child.

Share your beliefs with your child by starting with the basics and laying a foundation of truth. Avoid making statements that you may have to retract later. Be genuine in your explanation and consider how your words might be interpreted. If you share a concept that you have reservations about, your child will almost certainly detect your hesitation and become confused. They may also wonder about your truthfulness and be left questioning their own developing beliefs.

Terry's little brother, Billy, died recently of SIDS. Terry overheard you talking with a friend and heard them say, "God takes the angels to be with him" and "Now you have a guardian angel watching over you from heaven." Although you may have found some comfort in these statements, Terry clearly did not. She is angry with a God that would take her brother away from her. She is also worried that if she is good, God might take her, too. As a result, Terry begins to act out. In doing this, Terry is trying to make sure that God won't want her. She also is concerned about being watched from heaven. Does that mean Billy sees everything she does? Will he know if she plays in his room and uses his toys?

Your father died a few days ago, and today he was buried. You attended the events with your husband and four-year-old son, Danny. You are Catholic, and during the funeral service, Danny heard the priest talk about heaven. Having not heard this word before, Danny is now asking you what heaven is. You explain that after a person dies they go to heaven. Danny is quite confused, wondering how his grandpa could possibly be in heaven when he saw his body being buried in the ground earlier that day. You go on to explain that although the body remains buried, it is the soul that goes to heaven. Although Danny isn't quite sure about this, you have given him some basic information and can expand on this in future conversations.

Try to Maintain a Sense of Normalcy

Grieving children often experience their world as being in turmoil. To restore some semblance of security, try to follow your child's normal routine as closely as possible. This will bring structure and stability to an environment that seems completely out of control.

If you are overwhelmed and unable to adequately care for your child, consider having someone familiar to her come to your home to help you with her during this difficult time. This enables your child to be near you and to feel a part of what is happening, but relieves you of full responsibility for her care. If you send your child away, she may feel that her grief is unimportant because she is being excluded from sharing in the family's grief.

In the first few months following the death, try to avoid making any drastic changes (such as moving to a new home or starting your child in a new day care or school) unless it is absolutely necessary. These changes, despite their beneficial nature, can increase stress by adding to the burdens of change and loss the child has already experienced.

Use Available Resources and Seek Assistance

When grieving the death of a loved one, we sometimes feel completely overwhelmed, barely able to meet our own needs, much less provide adequately for the needs of our child. Communicate your needs to those around you and ask for the help that you need.

Initially, it may be helpful to have assistance attending to the details of the funeral or service. You may also receive offers to help with routine household tasks. Don't be afraid to accept these offers. People want to help, and these tasks provide them with a means for doing so. Consider what will be useful to you and your family, and then accept the offers that will be most helpful.

As time goes on, your needs will change. You may no longer require assistance with physical tasks, but now you may want a friend to listen attentively as you process the feelings that surface as the numbness begins to wear off. Whatever the case, remember that just as you may need assistance in your grief work, so too may your child.

There are a number of resources available to help children through the grieving process. Schools, churches, and local hospitals may offer children's grief support groups. Participation gives children an opportunity to learn more about grief, as well as ways to cope effectively with their feelings. In addition, when bereaved children get together, they become aware that they are not alone in their grief. They learn that other children have also experienced the death of someone close to them. It's one thing to hear that other children have experienced similar losses; it's quite another to sit in a room and talk with them. Although children may initially be somewhat reluctant to attend these groups, it has been my experience that they have usually benefited by participating in one.

Local bookstores and libraries have numerous books that can prepare us for our interactions with grieving children.

Some are designed to be read with your child. Others will be directed toward you as the adult. Still others are available for children to read independently.

The Internet is another source of information on this topic. It may also provide you with an opportunity for anonymous support through a chat room. Be sure to check into the verity of Internet resources and communication options. Web sites associated with established, nationally known organizations related to grieving are probably the best places to start.

Finally, counselors who specialize in grief can be helpful to both you and your child. While certainly not all children require individual counseling, it can become necessary. The feelings of grief are initially very intense. If they are faced and coped with effectively, however, the intensity will gradually ease. When the feelings remain intense for an extended period of time, additional intervention may be necessary.

If your child seems unable to live with the loss—as evidenced by the continuing intensity of her feelings and reactions to the death over an extended time—or if you have any questions or concerns, don't hesitate to call a trained professional. You could learn that your child is, in fact, grieving the death as one might expect, and that you are doing what you can to facilitate a healthy grieving process. Or, you might find that your child is having difficulties beyond what is considered within the norm, and intervention may be recommended. Either way, you can rest easier knowing that help is available to you and your child. There are others to share the grief journey with you.

Part Three
Approaching the Death
of a Child

6

When a Child Is Dying

This section provides guidance for situations in which children themselves are dying. Although it is painful to consider this topic, the unfortunate reality is that some children do die. Those who are dying are also grieving. Children who are dying are facing the ultimate loss—that of their own life. They are also grieving the impending loss of all the people, places, and things they love.

As a nurse and as a clinical social worker providing service in the area of pediatric hematology and oncology, I have worked extensively with children who have cancer or hematological illnesses. Although the great majority of these children are successfully treated, not all survive. During the past sixteen years, I have cared for a number of children in the final phase of their disease. I view this opportunity to serve as a privilege, and see myself as standing on sacred ground when working with these children. The care that I have given seems insignificant when I consider the lessons dying children have taught me about courage and strength, and the importance of living life fully, even in the face of death.

(In this section, I refer to the illness as cancer, as that has been my primary experience. It is, however, appropriate to apply this information to other circumstances involving children who are facing death.)

All seriously ill children, regardless of age or how much they have been told about their illness and prognosis, are aware to some degree of the gravity of their situation. For some, this awareness is a basic understanding; for others it goes much deeper. Children's awareness develops gradually over a period of time, often in relation to the progression of their illness and the implications for their lives.

Prior to their illness, these children likely entertained the innocent notion that everything that goes wrong can somehow be made "all better." The diagnosis of a life-threatening illness, however, brings with it some harsh realities. Mom and Dad can't always take away the hurt and make everything okay. Some things can penetrate even a parent's protective shield. Physicians—with their advanced knowledge, technology, and treatments—cannot cure all of life's diseases. And no matter how good these children might try to be, their cooperative behavior may not change the final outcome of their illness.

The initial hospitalization for diagnosis and subsequent admissions or outpatient clinic visits may overwhelm children, parents, and families. Numerous tests and procedures can be unfamiliar, uncomfortable, and may produce anxiety.

Parents anxiously await results that confirm the dreaded diagnosis of cancer or some other life-threatening condition. Children themselves—although they may not yet be informed of the significance of the events—know that something serious or unusual is taking place. Changes in their lives begin to make this very clear to them.

Changes in Daily Routine

A child with a life-threatening disease may spend a great deal of time in an environment that is unfamiliar and frightening. Her daily routine is disrupted. Naps and playtime may lose priority and have to be squeezed in only as treatment schedules allow. Sleep may be disturbed to take temperatures or give medications. Meals may be delayed or skipped, and diet is subject to change. Activities may be restricted depending on the child's physical condition.

Numerous physicians and other heath care professionals, many of them unfamiliar to the child, examine her. Nurses may perform tasks that have typically been done by parents, such as feeding, bathing, and changing diapers.

Siblings may stay at home with relatives or neighbors and might not be able to visit on a regular basis. The young patient often cannot attend school with her peers and may have a tutor instead. Contact with friends—often so important to children and teens—may be limited.

The child's world has been turned upside down. The security provided by the structure and predictability of daily routine is gone. Away from home—in another world, so to speak—the child is forced to adapt to a new, often chaotic, routine.

Hospital Stays

Children quickly figure out that going to the hospital is not like going to the clinic with a sore throat or earache. Hospitalization means not going home after seeing the doctor, and sometimes being separated from parents (for instance, during surgery).

The methods of giving medication to cancer patients are also unlike taking medicine for typical childhood ailments. Their condition often requires intravenous medications, so permanent intravenous lines are usually placed and the child is intermittently hooked up to IV pumps attached to a pole. Patients are told that the medications will help them to get better, yet—to a child—they do not appear to be working so well. In the past when they took medicine, such as an antibiotic for an ear infection, they soon felt better. These new medications, however, often make them feel even sicker (nausea and vomiting, for example, can be side effects of chemotherapy).

Finally, the child realizes rather quickly that health care providers mean business. The child may be offered a number of choices throughout the day, but does not have the option to refuse required treatment or care. The nurse may give the child the choice of juice or milk with her pill, but there is no question as to whether the pill will be taken.

Changes in Parental Behavior and Attitude

The parents of a dying child tend, at times, to be emotionally overwrought and tense. Their faces may be drawn and tight, often stained by tears. They may appear frightened and upset. These parents do not have all the answers; rather, they usually have numerous questions of their own. Hushed conversations in the hall with physicians or on the telephone with family and friends imply that they are hiding something.

Parents may come to be perceived by children as no longer being their protectors. The child is made to do unpleasant things, like cooperate in uncomfortable tests and procedures and take medications that do not taste good and have negative side effects.

At the same time, parents may become overindulgent. They may shower their child with gifts and seem ready to give them anything they want. Parents' expectations of their child can also change. They may, for example, accept behaviors that previously would not have been tolerated, such as hitting, kicking, screaming, and biting.

Finally, parents who would typically be at work may now be at the hospital. A mother may sleep at night in the child's hospital room, while fathers stay home with other children.

Changes in Body Image and Physical Abilities

Some medications have side effects that alter physical appearance. Weight loss or gain, hair loss, increased bruising, paleness, and mouth sores are just some of the side effects experienced by cancer patients.

A child may need different types of "tubes" or other medical equipment as a part of her care. She may also go through periods of time in which she is very tired, with little energy to engage in activities she usually enjoys. Whereas previously she could depend on her body to perform a certain way, it is no longer capable of doing some things.

With changes like these taking place, children develop a sense of how serious their condition has become. They need only look in the mirror or consider their physical limitations to see the signals.

Changes in the Condition of Other Patients

Play is a central activity in children's lives. It remains important even in the face of serious illness and hospitalization. Children's hospitals and clinics often have Child Life Specialists on staff who provide educational and general play opportunities to promote normal growth and development. Through play, children can experiment with some of the mechanical aspects of their illness (central IV line, feeding tube) and develop an understanding of their body, their disease, and the necessary treatments.

Children often socialize with other patients during play activities. Friendships can be forged as children talk about their illnesses and treatments. As a result, when one of them takes a turn for the worse, the other children soon realize that something is not quite right. Maybe they aren't seeing their friend at the clinic or in the hospital anymore. Or per-haps—when they did see their friend last—she looked very, very sick and was uninterested or unable to play. Or maybe they overheard the health care providers or their parents talking about the child.

Children tend to be keenly observant of all that is going on in their environment. If they are not told what is happen-ing, they will form their own conclusions based on what they have seen and heard. If and when they conclude that their friend has died, the seriousness of their own illness will take on an added dimension. They may now begin to wonder about the possibility of their own death.

Changes in Their Own Condition

When children initially achieve a remission from their dis-ease, they may be lulled into a false sense of security as life reverts to some semblance of what it used to be. But this security can be shattered by a relapse or recurrence. The child's daily routine must again accommodate illness, and hospitalization is often necessary. Seeing her parents' response to events, as well as additional changes in her phys-ical condition, the child becomes even more aware that something serious or unusual is happening.

If the disease does not respond to treatment, or side effects threaten the child's already fragile condition, she becomes even more aware of the gravity of her circumstances.

Parents confer with physicians to discuss options. A deci-sion to pursue further aggressive treatment might cause the child to become critically ill. Her condition might necessitate a transfer to an intensive care unit, where she will be surrounded by medical equipment that sustains her life and monitors her condition.

On the other hand, the focus of care may shift from aggressive attempts to cure to a plan that addresses comfort and quality of life. Unnecessary treatments and procedures will be reduced, if not entirely eliminated. The child might be taken home, with the intent of living as fully as possible until the time of death.

As a child moves closer to death, her physical condition can continue to change. She may tire more easily, which means she will become less active. She may lose control of various bodily functions (bowel and bladder, movement and sensation) and exhibit little or no interest in food or drink. Pain management may require significant medication, which can also cause sleepiness and inactivity. Again, changes such as these must be handled openly and honestly with the child.

Ideally, the child will be involved—at least to some extent—in the discussions between the physicians and her parents. If she is not, however, it should not be concluded that she is unaware of the significance of all that is happening. Children can add up the different signals and figure out that they are not getting better, that they are, in fact, dying.

Children—given their awareness of the circumstances—need to talk about the situation. If parents are unable to discuss it with them, others who are able to respond to this need must be made available.

Stages of Dying

We noted earlier that Elisabeth Kübler-Ross's pioneering work with terminally ill people identified five stages of the dying process: denial, anger, bargaining, depression, and acceptance. Although these are typically applied to adults, dying children can also experience them. Very young children may not understand that they are dying, but older ones gradually realize what is happening. Like adults, they do not necessarily move through the stages in the order just presented; many exhibit one or more stages simultaneously, and they may experience them more than once in the process of dying.

The first stage, denial, is experienced by almost all dying people—not only at the time of the initial diagnosis, but throughout the progression of the illness. Denial functions as a buffer in that it can provide a brief respite from an overwhelming situation. It enables the patient to adjust to the painful reality and find additional coping strategies.

When denial can no longer be maintained, it may be replaced by feelings of anger, rage, envy, and resentment. The terminally ill person asks, "Why me?" She may lash out in many directions and project anger onto almost anything in her environment at random.

The third stage, bargaining, can be helpful for brief periods of time. If people have been unable to face the sad facts in the first stage, and have been angry with people and God in the second, maybe—they reason—they can succeed in making some sort of an agreement to postpone the inevitable.

When terminally ill patients can no longer deny their situation, their numbness, anger, and bargaining may soon be replaced with a sense of loss and depression. Dying people are in the process of losing everybody and everything they love. If they express their sorrow, acceptance will likely come easier.

Kübler-Ross suggested that if people have the time and opportunity to work through their feelings, most will reach a stage of acceptance during which they are neither angry nor depressed about their fate. It is as if their pain is gone, their struggle is over, and the person rests before the journey ahead.

These stages of dying have often been applied to the grief process. Upon learning of the death of a loved one, many of us can remember the initial shock, followed later by anger, depression, and at some point, an acceptance of sorts. It is important to remember, however, that adults and children alike do not move through death or grief in a completely predictable manner. People often experience several emotions at the same time. They may feel a sense of peace one day, only to find their sense of loss unresolved the next. Grief is an individual process, influenced by a variety of factors. In moving toward the ultimate acceptance of death—the point at which it becomes integrated into the reality of one's life— many people feel that for every few steps forward, there is another step back.

7

Concerns of Dying Children

*C*hildren who are dying will understandably have concerns. If you have an understanding of what these are, you will be in a better position to listen and respond to them.

Fear of Abandonment and Isolation

Children in the terminal stage of an illness will often worry about being abandoned, not only by members of their health care team, but also by their friends and families. They may find that the doctors are not coming by as frequently as they had been or that their favorite nurse has not dropped in for a surprise visit lately. Their friends may not come around as much, in spite of invitations to visit. Even family members may become too busy to spend time talking and playing.

Whether the change is conscious or unconscious, intentional or unintentional, the effect is the same. The children—noting the difference in the interactions—may begin to fear that they will be alone at the time of their death.

A child may sense that others feel uncomfortable in her presence, knowing that she is going to die. Given this, the child may try to hide obvious symptoms that draw attention to her condition. It is as if she is attempting to ensure that she will not be abandoned.

In the following examples, children sense the discomfort of a family member or friend and alter their behavior in an effort to protect others from the pain and sadness associated with their impending death. In doing this, the child tries to stave off the sense of being abandoned by making it easier for others to continue to visit and be present.

Adam, a ten-year-old in the terminal stage of leukemia, noticed that his mom would start crying and make an excuse to leave the room whenever he asked what was going to happen to him. He had overheard the doctors talking to her and knew that he was not going to get better. Adam desperately wanted to discuss this with his mom, but after a while he figured out that it was too difficult for her. He very much wanted his mother to be with him, so Adam decided not to mention his concerns about dying to her. He hoped that if he didn't talk about them, his mom would feel comfortable enough to stay with him no matter what happened.

Sixteen-year-old Emily had recently relapsed—yet again—and it became quickly apparent that she would not survive her disease. Over time, Emily noticed that her friends weren't visiting much anymore, and when they did, they barely said anything to her. She noted that they seemed particularly uncomfortable when she wasn't up and dressed for their visits.

As a result, whenever her friends were coming, Emily made an extra effort to look as best as she could. No matter how miserable she might be feeling, Emily would get up, get dressed, put on her wig, and even apply some makeup. Not wanting to be cut off from her friends, Emily was willing to be uncomfortable in an effort to have her friends feel more comfortable and, therefore, more willing to visit.

Children who are dying may also feel isolated from the world and people at large. Not only do friends and family members visit less frequently, when they do come they don't talk with the children the way they used to.

In the past, visitors would relate stories about what was happening in their lives—what was going on at home and in school, who won the baseball game, what they were planning to wear to a party, what activities they had planned for the coming weekend. As the illness progresses—and the reality of impending death becomes more apparent—people don't seem to know what to talk about. It is almost as if they are afraid to discuss the events of everyday life because they know the child won't be alive to enjoy them much longer and it's painful to think of a future without them.

Although reminders of a lost future may sadden these children, it probably hurts more to be excluded from the present world. They may not have much time left, but they are still alive. If these children want to continue to participate in certain activities, attempts should be made to accommodate them. Certainly children will face limitations, but usually the pleasure of being involved will more than compensate.

For as long as Jody could remember, she had been going to watch her older brother play in various sporting activities. Although her physical condition now prevented her from being able to attend the games, Jody remained interested in how her brother played and the outcomes of the games.

As time passed, however, Jody noticed that her brother didn't talk about the games unless she specifically initiated the conversation. When asked how this made her feel, Jody indicated she was hurt and angry. She was beginning to wonder if he even loved her anymore, and felt as if he were waiting for her to die.

Jody's brother, on the other hand, said he didn't think she would care about his games anymore. They seemed insignificant in light of her impending death. After talking about this with Jody, however, he realized how important they were to her. The sporting events represented something special they could share together. By telling her how he and his team were doing, he enabled Jody to continue to be a part of his life.

Fear of Retribution

It seems to be human nature to find someone or something to blame when a situation goes wrong. It is difficult to understand and accept that a disease just happened for some unexplained reason. Younger children in particular tend to engage in magical thinking, which means that those with life-threatening illnesses may believe that something they thought, said, or did somehow caused their situation to occur. Children may, therefore, review their past to determine what—if anything—could be responsible.

The fear that disease is the result of some form of retribution is evident in the following examples:

Twelve-year-old Joey firmly believed that he became sick with cancer because he had stolen candy from a store. It didn't matter to Joey that his parents had reprimanded him or that he had returned the candy to the store. Somehow that was not enough. In Joey's mind, he was being punished for his behavior.

In a discussion about the situation, Joey shared that he imagined God to be a loving and forgiving God. Clearly, however, Joey did not believe this to be true for him as he continued to maintain that he was being punished for his past mistake. Joey needed to blame someone, so he blamed himself. It had to be his fault. Why else would he be dying? Why else would he have gotten sick in the first place? This had to be how God was punishing him.

Missy, a six-year-old with recurrent lymphoma, was sure that she had relapsed because she hadn't taken all of her pills as she had been instructed. After all, her mom and the nurses had told her repeatedly, "If you take all of your medicine like a good girl, you'll get well again."

Missy had never confided to anyone about the pill she had spit out once when the nurse wasn't looking. Surely it was because she had not taken this one pill that the cancer had come back and she was now dying.

Fifteen-year-old Tony was convinced that he was dying because, as he said, "I didn't want to get better bad enough." It was a part of Tony's family's religious beliefs that if you want something badly and pray enough about it, then you will get it. It followed then, that if Tony had really wanted to get well again, he would have recovered. If he had prayed enough, he wouldn't be dying.

Fear of Dying and Death

Dying children often have fears associated with the dying process, as well as with death itself. They wonder, for example, what it will be like. Will they be in pain? Will they lose control of their bodily functions? Will they be conscious, aware of what is happening to them? Will it be scary? Who, if anyone, will be there with them? What will happen after death? What will become of their physical bodies? How will they get to heaven? Will they know anyone there?

Mike, age fifteen, was first diagnosed with bone cancer at the age of twelve. He underwent aggressive chemotherapy *for the better part of two years. After completing his initial treatment, Mike was in remission for almost a year. When the cancer recurred, a new treatment plan was developed, but Mike's response to it was disappointing.*

Mike and his parents soon realized that he was not going to be cured. Together they made the decision to continue with therapy for as long as it was helping to keep the disease in check without significant adverse affects. The goal was to provide Mike with some quality time in which he could continue to do the things that were most important to him. Mike and his parents were, however, realistic about the expected outcome and discussed it openly with one another.

The cancer ultimately spread to Mike's lungs, causing breathing difficulties. Aggressive therapy was discontinued, and Mike chose to return home, where he planned to remain until he died. But Mike was anxious about how he would die. He had a particular fear of suffocation. Mike was reassured that everything possible would be done to keep him comfortable with medications and oxygen.

As his condition deteriorated, Mike became increasingly anxious. He made the decision to return to the hospital, as that is where he felt most comfortable. When Mike arrived, he appeared quite distressed. In a relatively short period of time, however, he visibly relaxed. Within several hours, Mike died a peaceful death, surrounded by his family and several close friends.

Seventeen-year-old Amy—diagnosed two years previously with cancer—was now in the end stage of her disease. Although she appeared to accept the fact of her impending death, Amy complained bitterly about the indignities that would accompany it.

Over the last few days of her hospitalization, Amy had lost movement and sensation from the waist down, as well as the ability to control her bowel and bladder functions.

Although Amy had always taken pride in being able to care for herself, she began to fear that even this would gradually become impossible.

As she grew more dependent on others for care that was becoming more and more difficult, Amy considered herself to be a burden to her mom. At one point she even said, "It's bad enough that I have to go through this, Mom, but it's even worse that you do, too!" Amy apologized repeatedly to her mom for the situation, as if she were somehow responsible for it.

The health care team did their best to acknowledge and respect Amy's continuing need for privacy and dignity, striving to let her do what she could for herself. Ultimately, Amy learned to work with her limitations and was able to return home to live for about a month before she died quietly in her sleep.

By the same token, some children move beyond fear and begin to anticipate their death. They begin to view death in less fearful, more positive terms. This acceptance is evident in the following examples:

Peter—barely four years old—wondered aloud what it would be like in heaven. His startled mother—not knowing quite what else to say—quickly replied, "I don't know, Peter. What do you think it will be like?"

Peter thought about it for a while and then looked at his mother and said, "There won't be any more pokes, and I'll see my friends with cancer again. But we won't be sick anymore!"

Four-year-old Kathy told her mom not to worry about her after she died. Kathy's grandfather had died within the last year, and she believed that he was in heaven. Kathy assured her mother that Grandpa was waiting to greet her in heaven and that he would help to take care of her until her mom was able to join them both there.

8

Concerns of the Parents

*P*arents of children who are dying often share many of the same concerns as the children themselves. Understanding these fears can be useful as you care for these children and their families.

Fear of Abandonment or Isolation

Just as children sometimes fear abandonment in their dying process, parents may also be concerned about being left alone.

When their children are dying, parents typically need to talk about the situation as they struggle to come to terms with it. Unfortunately, however, parents often discover that the people they thought they could turn to for help may be unable to respond to their need because the subject of death, particularly when it involves children, makes many people thoroughly uncomfortable.

Rather than face their own fears and concerns, potential supporters might gradually quit calling or visiting. If they do continue to come around, they may deny the impending death, choosing to change the subject, or leave whenever anyone mentions it. This can leave parents without support at a time when they are already quite vulnerable.

Parents can, of course, seek professional counseling at such times, but this may or may not address the sense of isolation. It may feel as if their world has stopped, while for others it has continued to move forward. Although the parents' time and energy obviously has to be focused on the needs of their dying child, they benefit greatly from knowing that others have not forgotten them. There will come a time when they re-enter the world again—when they try to resume life as they once knew it—and it will be helpful for them to know that people will be available to assist them in this process.

Fear of Failure in the Role of Parent and Protector

Parents of children who are dying often wonder if they are in some way responsible for the situation. They may question, "If only I had taken her to the doctor sooner, maybe the treatment would have worked better, maybe the outcome would have been different. Why did I think she had the flu?" or "Maybe she got sick because we live in the city with all the smog and pollution. Why did I ever agree to take this new job and move?"

Parents—like their children—want to know the whys, hows, and whats of all that is taking place. It seems easier to cope, somehow, if they can understand why it is happening and where they can focus the blame, rather than simply accepting that the disease just happened for some unknown reason.

Parents may also feel they have failed their children in some way. After all, parents are supposed to be able to protect their children from the bad things that can happen in life. Does their child's illness mean that they have failed somehow in their parental responsibilities?

Parents are beset by many questions during a child's terminal illness: How do we know if we will be able to make the right decisions regarding treatment and care? How can we be sure that the benefits of therapy will outweigh the side effects and potential complications? Should we allow the doctor to use an experimental drug or procedure? Will we know if and when we have done enough for our child? Will there come a time when discontinuing aggressive, cure-oriented treatment is the best decision for our child? How will we know where our child should die? Would it be better to be at home as a family or to be in the hospital where assistance is more readily available? How will we live with our decisions and the implications of them? What if we get new information later that makes us second-guess an earlier decision? Will that mean we have failed in our role of parent and protector?

Fear of Coping with a Child's Dying Process

Parents may wonder how they will be able to endure watching their child suffer and die. A sense of helplessness is common. Having actively cared for their child through many changes and circumstances, parents may now feel inadequate to meet their child's many needs. They may become focused on their inability to change the ultimate outcome. In this case, they need help in redirecting their attention to those things they can continue to do for as long as their child is alive: talking with her, reading a special story, listening to a soothing tape, cuddling in bed, massaging her hands and feet, preparing a favorite food.

At the same time, however, parents may feel guilty for thinking of their own pain and inadequacy when considering what their children are facing. They may question the kind of parents they are if they have trouble handling the situation.

There may come a time when parents see death as almost a blessing because it will bring an end to their child's pain and suffering. This admission, however, may overwhelm parents with guilt. They may wonder how to live with themselves when praying for the death of a child. Will other people be able to understand that although they never wanted their children to be sick in the first place, there can come a time—in the course of an illness—when death provides the only release? Will people be able to accept them with all their confusing thoughts and emotions?

9
Providing Care
to Dying Children

*C*hildren with terminal diseases live in a world that is, in a sense, becoming smaller and more focused as they prepare for and finally enter the actual dying process. Ideally, they are being cared for by people they know and love, in a setting that is comfortable and suited to their needs. Their attention and energy is likely limited, and best conserved, therefore, for activities that have the most meaning for them (reading a story with a parent, playing a game with a brother or sister, or visiting with a friend).

In this chapter and the next, we will survey the ways caregivers can facilitate this process for children and their families. The term caregiver refers in this context to health care professionals involved in the care of dying children, as distinct from parents or other primary caretakers. This information, while addressed to caregivers, is valuable as well for family members and friends of the families of children who are dying.

Provide Consistent Caregivers

Whenever possible—whether the child is at home, in a hospital, or in a hospice—it is helpful to provide consistent caregivers. The presence of unfamiliar caregivers can be highly stressful for a child and her family at a time when they are already vulnerable.

A caregiver who knows the child is in a better position to anticipate and respond to her needs. Through familiarity, caregivers come to sense the rhythms of the child and family; they understand what is or is not important to them, what has or has not been helpful, and what the child likes and dislikes.

It is always imperative for care plans to be complete and accurate in case an unfamiliar caregiver needs to take over, and that alternate caregivers are quickly accessible if necessary. Good planning facilitates new caregivers who need to step in and provide high quality care. It also conveys to the child and family that their overall well-being is fully considered.

Emphasize That the Children Have Done Nothing Wrong

It is important that dying children feel loved and cared for. They may be questioning why this is happening and wondering if somehow they are to blame. Explore their thoughts and ideas and try to correct any misconceptions they might have.

If children are firmly convinced that they are in some way responsible for their illness—because of something they thought, said, or did—you may be unable to convince them otherwise. Continue to express your unconditional regard for them; assure them you will be there for them no matter what. Gently attempt to dissuade them from believing they are to blame, but don't force the issue. If you push too hard, children may shut down and refuse to talk about their concerns and fears. This will alienate them at a time they are very much in need of your care and support.

Communicate with Honesty

Most children don't ask a question without expecting some type of answer. As a caregiver, if a question is asked, it is your responsibility to answer it. Consider carefully the issue or concern that has been raised, and take care to answer only what is being asked. Use language children can understand and avoid burdening them with information they have not requested.

Children do not always ask direct questions. They may ask seemingly unrelated questions, make statements, or even take actions that indirectly indicate their understanding or awareness of the situation, as illustrated by the following example:

Allison, a fourteen-year-old girl with lymphoma, asked me, "What happens if this chemo doesn't work?" I had been Allison's primary nurse for more than six months, and during this time, we had developed a trusting relationship. I knew Allison did not have any further options for curative treatment and was comfortable exploring the issue with her. I decided to direct the question back to Allison by asking, "What do you think will happen if this chemo doesn't work?" She replied by rephrasing her original question in a way that directly addressed her immediate concerns: "I know there are only so many treatment options available. I also know I've used all of them but the one I'm taking right now. So, if this doesn't work, does it mean I'm going to die?"

Eleven-year-old Mark, in the end stage of leukemia, asked to do his Christmas shopping early. Christmas was his favorite holiday, and he wanted to be prepared for it. Although it was only October, his parents honored his request. Mark spent an afternoon at the mall selecting gifts. When he got home, Mark wrapped and labeled the presents, then put them in his closet. Within a week his condition worsened, and Mark died several days later.

Other questions and comments that speak to the children's awareness of their condition include:

- Who will get my toys?
- Do you think my friends will remember me?
- I wonder if Grandpa will recognize me in heaven without my hair?
- I wonder what it would have been like to graduate.

All of these questions and comments reflect sincere thought and deserve honest responses. When addressing them with these children, be aware of your nonverbal communication—body language, tone of voice, eye contact—so as to avoid conveying a message you don't intend.

Facilitate Communication as Appropriate

Gently encourage and model honest communication among children, families, and caregivers. Do not, however, force this communication. If a child has difficulty speaking directly with her physicians, she may ask you as her caregiver to raise the questions for her. Or, if she senses that her parents are uncomfortable talking with her about her fears and concerns, she may look to you—a trusted caregiver—to listen. She may also ask that you talk with her parents about their discomfort and let them know how much she wants to be able to share her thoughts and feelings with them.

Some parents use denial as a means of coping with the situation. It is important for caregivers to recognize denial as a coping mechanism. Caregivers can encourage parents to handle the situation differently, but cannot force them to do so. Some people appear to hang on to denial regardless of the circumstances. If this is the case, it is particularly helpful to pay attention to the implications of this denial for the child. Be aware of her needs and ensure that they are addressed—if not by the parents, then by another relative or caregiver.

The following examples illustrate how parents use denial to protect either themselves or their child from the painful reality of the situation. In one case, the parent was unable to let go of her denial, and her son died without having an opportunity to speak openly with her. In the other, the parents were able to recognize their daughter's need to communicate directly with them, and they engaged in honest dialogue with her about her illness and impending death.

Chris, now sixteen, had been diagnosed with leukemia when he was twelve years old. For many years, his mother, a single parent, had used alcohol as a way of coping in life. Chris and his mom lived out of town, which meant that his mother often brought him to the hospital and then went home until he was ready to be discharged. Sometimes, when Chris was very ill, she would stay in town at a hotel. Even then, however, she spent little time at the hospital with Chris. She seemed to be either at the hotel sleeping or in a bar somewhere. Often she would call late at night—after an evening of drinking—to check and see how he was doing.

Chris learned to accept his mother's behavior, acknowledging that it probably wasn't going to change. Although he knew that she loved him, Chris recognized that she was unable to deal with the situation or offer him much comfort or support. Rather than expecting her to meet his needs, Chris learned to turn to others for help. In the process, he grew particularly close to one of the doctors and several of the nurses.

When it became apparent that he was dying, Chris tried a final time to reach out to his mom. She was, however, unable to respond, seeming to spend even less time with him than she had previously. Chris knew that if he wanted support, he would again have to look for it from someone other than his mother. As much as she loved him, Chris realized she couldn't face the thought of being with him when he died.

On the night before Chris's death, his mom called to say she wouldn't be coming to visit if he thought he would be okay. Chris told her he'd be all right and indicated he planned to see her later. Soon after, his condition began to deteriorate. When asked if he wanted staff to try to reach his mother, Chris said no, asking instead that the doctor and nurses he had grown close to be called. Within hours after they arrived, Chris died, surrounded by people who had loved and cared for him throughout his illness. They had, in a way, become his surrogate family.

When his mother came to the hospital—several hours after her son's death—she was able to go in and spend some time saying good-bye to him. Upon arriving that day and hearing that Chris had died, she had said, "If only I had known he was so sick, I would have come to visit."

Chris's caregivers knew how difficult it had been for his mom to deal not only with his illness, but with the fact of the inevitable moment of his death. They assured her that Chris had not been alone and that he had died comfortably and peacefully. In his own way, Chris appeared to have chosen to protect his mother from various aspects of his illness and, ultimately, from the moment of his death. She, in turn, was able let him go by spending time with him following his death.

When Rebecca, now seven, had been diagnosed with bone cancer two years earlier, her parents had informed her that something was wrong with her bones, choosing deliberately not to use the word cancer. In their minds, saying that someone had cancer was the equivalent of saying they were going to die. They believed that if they could prevent Rebecca from hearing the word, somehow they could prevent her from realizing how sick she was.

But Rebecca was quite aware of her situation. Although she hadn't heard her parents say the word cancer to her, she did overhear it from others. She was tuned in to her parents' behavior, and could tell from it that something was very wrong. The changes in her physical condition were further evidence of the seriousness of her situation.

As desperately as her parents wanted to protect her from the truth, they could not. In making the decisions they did, Rebecca's parents conveyed a strong message that it was not okay to talk about what was happening. Without intending it, her parents forced Rebecca to turn to others for information and support.

Fortunately for Rebecca and her parents, the hospital staff was able to point out to the parents the extent of Rebecca's understanding of her situation. When enough specific examples of her awareness were presented, they were able to put aside their own fears and engage openly in discussions with their daughter. Although they couldn't change the fact of her illness, Rebecca's parents were ultimately able to support her in the dying process.

Acknowledge and Encourage Expression of Feelings

In providing care to dying children, it is beneficial not only to acknowledge their feelings, but to encourage the expression of them as well. Assure the child that whatever she is feeling is okay, and let her know how helpful it can be to share those feelings with other people.

The most effective way to communicate this message is through example. Share your feelings with the child, knowing that she in turn may feel more comfortable bringing up her feelings with you or someone else. You might, for example, say, "It hurts me to see you so sick, Jenna. I wish that I could make you better, but I can't. I can see that you are sad, and I want to help you with that. Do you want to talk about it?"

Some parents may choose not to share their feelings with their child. They may assume their child is too young or immature to understand the significance of what is happening and intentionally avoid discussing it with them. Others' parents may feel they need to be strong for their child, and take great effort in trying to hide their emotions from them. Without intending it, these parents may be sending a message that it is not okay to talk about one's feelings.

In either case, caregivers can help the situation by carefully addressing a child's feelings—in the presence of her parents. You could, for example, say, "Mary, you have asked me a number of times about how sick you are, and I know you're scared about what is going to happen. I imagine you might want to talk with your mom and dad about this, and I can help you do that if you want."

In doing this, you have pointed out to the parents that their child does in fact have an awareness of what is happening. You have also acknowledged the child's feelings related to her situation and opened the door for communication between the child and her parents. Ideally the parents will follow your example, sharing their feelings more openly while also conveying a willingness to listen.

Keep the Child Comfortable

Children who are dying often have concerns about how they will die and if they will be in pain. It is important to talk about these fears and let the children know that, although you are not sure exactly how they will die, you will do everything you can to keep them as comfortable as possible.

In addition to medications, a number of other methods can be utilized to address pain, including distraction techniques, guided imagery, meditation, music therapy, aromatherapy, and gentle massage. Keeping children as pain-free as possible alleviates some of the fear and anxiety they may have regarding their impending death.

Allow Children to Make Choices and Maintain Independence

It is important for children to feel that they have some control over choices that have an impact on them. They also derive significant satisfaction from being able to do things for themselves.

The fact that a child is dying does not make these sources of satisfaction disappear. In fact, it may become even more important to allow for choices and independence, when appropriate, in light of the situation. As a child gets closer to death, she may feel as if more and more in her world is out of her control. She may also become increasingly dependent upon others as her physical condition declines and the need for care increases.

Caregivers can offer children opportunities, when appropriate, to make choices about their care. Encourage children to continue to participate in their care, emphasizing those things they can still do for themselves rather than focusing on what they can no longer do. The importance of doing this is illustrated in the following example:

Randy was fifteen years old when his cancer recurred for the third and final time. He had always been a fairly private child who seemed to benefit from quiet time alone each day. Randy was also fiercely independent and took pride in his ability to care for himself during much of his illness. He knew, however, that although he was fully capable of caring for himself now, over time he would become more and more dependent on others.

Randy's caregivers worked hard to ensure that Randy could make appropriate choices throughout his day. They assisted Randy in developing his daily schedule. He was able to negotiate certain aspects of his care and set limits on how he wanted to spend his time. Randy made choices about when he wanted to get cleaned up for the day, what he wanted to eat, who he wanted to see, and when he wanted to see them.

Given his private nature, Randy requested that he not be disturbed for an hour in the morning and another hour in the afternoon. He also asked to post a sign on his door, directing visitors to the nurse to verify if he was feeling up to seeing people. When staff entered his room, particular attention was paid to knocking before entering. They also attempted to group Randy's procedures as much as possible so as to minimize the number of times they went in and out of the room.

As Randy grew increasingly dependent on others for his care, consistent caregivers were provided as much as possible. By having people who were familiar with him, Randy avoided having to repeatedly inform people regarding his care. Primary caregivers gave him the time to do for himself what he could—painstaking as it might be for Randy—and respectfully took care of his other needs.

By helping Randy to maintain some sense of control in his life, he was able to adapt to his situation as it changed without focusing on its negative aspects.

Determine Goals and Allow
for Hope in Achieving Them

It is common for people of all ages, when facing the reality of their own death, to have certain things they want to accomplish before they die. Caregivers working with dying children direct a great deal of effort toward helping them to live as fully as possible for the remainder of their lives. Part of this involves being aware of what is important and meaningful to them, and helping to determine what, if any, goals they might have that you can assist them in achieving.

For some children, the wishes are fairly simple (visiting with a grandparent who is coming from out of town), while for others they are more involved (a trip to Disney World). Whether or not a goal can be met—and the manner in which this is done—will obviously be influenced by a number of factors. In some situations it may be necessary to find creative ways to assist children in completing their goals. The following examples illustrate how this can be done:

Brittany was soon to finish kindergarten when her leukemia recurred. Although she started aggressive therapy almost immediately, it became apparent rather quickly that her body was not responding.

Brittany had eagerly anticipated going to kindergarten and it was obvious to everyone how much she enjoyed being there. She excelled academically and socially and was devastated when her physical condition made it too difficult to be at school.

Given Brittany's strong desire to complete kindergarten with her classmates, the school and her mom developed a plan to help her achieve this goal. Brittany's class made graduation cards, and several of her friends, along with their teacher, presented these to her along with a video copy of the class graduation ceremony.

Although Brittany wasn't able to participate in the way she had initially imagined she would, her desire to finish kindergarten was identified and accommodated.

Tommy was almost four when he became critically ill with a fungal infection related to the intense treatment he was receiving for his lymphoma. He had been planning to have a big birthday celebration with a group of his friends and was extremely disappointed when it appeared that it would have to be delayed, if not cancelled.

Tommy had been hospitalized for several weeks when the decision was made to discontinue aggressive therapy and transfer him from the intensive care unit to the patient care area where he had been hospitalized numerous times throughout his illness.

Although Tommy continued to be gravely ill—and it was apparent that he would not live much longer—his condition appeared to stabilize for a brief period. Tommy's parents knew how important it was for him to celebrate his birthday with his friends, so they acted quickly and arranged to have his party at the hospital a few weeks earlier than had previously been planned. Everyone enjoyed the celebration and Tommy spent the next several weeks reliving the special time he had shared with his friends.

Tommy died the day after his fourth birthday.

Explore the Concept of Heaven (When Appropriate)

While caring for a dying child, caregivers may learn what that child believes about what happens when a person dies. If a child believes in life after death and the concept of heaven, it may be appropriate to explore what the child imagines heaven will be like. If she asks, "What will it be like in heaven?" an appropriate response might be, "What do you think it will be like?" The child has probably given this considerable thought, and will likely give you a fairly detailed idea of what she believes it will be like and who will be there to greet her.

Children are often eager to share their imaginings and appreciate when someone can respond to this need and listen attentively to their questions and concerns. Discussing this topic with children can ease some of their anxiety, as well as provide them with something to move toward.

If, for example, Zachary views heaven as a happy place where there is no more pain and where people who have died are reunited, he will likely be less fearful of the dying process. He may envision a loved one—perhaps a grandparent—who awaits him in heaven with God.

In exploring the concept of heaven with children and their families, it is imperative to note that there is a distinct difference between listening to a person's freely shared beliefs and actively initiating a conversation so as to discuss one's own. It is inappropriate to impose personal beliefs, but it can be quite beneficial to facilitate the expression of the beliefs of a dying child.

Give the Children Permission to Die

At times, children may worry about how painful their death will be for their family and friends. Expression of this concern may be the child's way of asking for permission to die. Acknowledge her concern while at the same time emphasizing that her needs are most important now.

If parents are unsure about how to respond to their child when this issue arises, model ways to respond for them. Say, for example, "I can see that you are worried about your family, Lisa. They love you very, very much and will miss you dearly when you are gone. I know, however, that they will always remember you and that they will have a special place in their heart for you." Or, "It's hard to see you struggling so much. You've been living with this illness for a long time and now it's time to rest. It's okay to let go."

10

Providing Care to Parents

$\mathcal{J}$ust as there are certain things that caregivers can do to assist children in their dying process, the same is true when extending care to their families.

Make Specific Offers and Follow through on Them

Most families are grateful to people who make genuine offers of assistance during this difficult time. Although they might not need anything at the time an offer is made, parents take comfort in knowing who they can call if something comes up.

Having said this, however, it is important to note that there are families who may have difficulty asking for or accepting assistance. Perhaps they are accustomed to taking care of things themselves or feel as if they have taken up too much of other people's time already. If parents have these issues, it might be helpful to reframe the situation for them. Point out that they had no control over the situation they are in and emphasize that they will not be in this position permanently. It may also help to note that if someone else were in need, it is likely they would be more than willing to offer their assistance.

It is not uncommon for extended family members and friends to ask caregivers what they can do to assist children and their families. Describe examples of help that other families have found beneficial and encourage these people to consider offering that kind of help. Inform them that rather than leaving a family hanging with a generic offer to do something, it is very helpful to be specific about what they are willing and able to do. In this way, the bulk of the burden of responding to an offer is removed from the family. Parents are clear as to what has been offered and aren't left wondering if it would be okay to ask about a specific task. If parents decline help initially, suggest that these friends touch base with them periodically to see how they are doing and offer assistance again. This demonstrates their genuine concern and sends a message to the parents and children that they have not been forgotten.

If an offer of assistance is extended, it is important to follow through and do whatever has been offered. Parents are vulnerable and need to have people they can rely on. Now is not the time for them to be disappointed when offers they have counted on fall apart.

Provide Support, Not Answers

Parents have undoubtedly been asking themselves again and again why this is happening and what they might have done to cause it. Acknowledge that situations like this are extremely difficult to accept and sometimes even harder to understand.

Avoid placing blame on the parents for their children's illness or burdening them with theories as to why it might have happened. At this time, there isn't anything anyone can say or do to change the final outcome, and there is nothing to be gained in weighing parents down with ideas that may or may not have validity. Parents look to caregivers for support, and it is support, not speculation and theorizing, that should be provided.

Affirm Parents' Love and Capability

Parents of children who are dying are in an extremely difficult situation—one they certainly would never have chosen for themselves or their family. It is critical to offer encouragement. Recognize that they are doing the best they can under the circumstances. Affirm them as loving, nurturing parents, capable of making decisions that are in their children's best interests. Reassure them that they have not failed as parents and protectors. Cancer is a disease that can happen to anyone. It is not something they could have protected their child against.

Once cancer touches a family, numerous decisions must be made. Parents can become overwhelmed, wondering how they will ever be able to make the right decisions. If asked, assist parents in gathering the information necessary to make the best decisions. Assure them that there are no right or wrong answers. Emphasize that they are doing the best they can with the information available.

Accept Parents Where They Are in Their Process

It can be devastating for parents to watch their children suffer and die and to deal with the overwhelming sense of powerlessness that accompanies the experience. Commend parents for the ways they have provided comfort and support to their children. Offer suggestions regarding things they can continue to do now, even in the face of the impending death (rocking the child, sharing favorite memories, listening to a special tape or watching a favorite movie, arranging for a best friend to visit, stroking their hair, lotioning their skin). Focus on what parents can do. This alleviates some of their sense of helplessness.

Help parents see how well they have handled many challenging situations throughout their child's illness. Gently reassure them that somehow they will manage to get through this as well. Remind parents to take care of themselves, too, so they will have the strength necessary to meet their child's needs. Encourage them to ask for and accept the help they need.

Finally, accept and support the parents where they are in their process. They need this more than anything else. Remain objective while encouraging them to share their thoughts and feelings. Although you might think you would do things differently if you were the parent, this is irrelevant. Part of the caregiver's role is to ensure that parents have access to information that enables them to make informed decisions regarding their child's care. Once decisions have been made, it is critical to support them. Second-guessing parents' decisions in any way at this time would be highly inappropriate.

Every situation is unique, and families will make the decisions they feel are best for their children. People don't choose to have cancer enter their lives. But when it does, they do the best they can in a difficult situation. Although they did not choose the diagnosis, they can make choices as to how they will live with it and, in some cases, how they will die with it. Caregivers must support and accept these decisions, recognizing that they required much thought and anguish.

Conclusion

$\mathcal{W}$e all know that death is a part of the mystery of life, but we never know exactly when or how it will enter and touch our lives. Children today may reach adulthood without ever experiencing the death of someone close to them. Unless adequately prepared, they will have difficulty coping with a death when it occurs. As parents, teachers, and health professionals, it is our responsibility to prepare children for the inevitable losses in life by introducing the concept of death at an early age.

Children are naturally inquisitive about death, just as they are about life. It makes sense, then, that we seek to educate them regarding it. Children are eager to learn. If we convey the message that it is not okay to talk about death, they will simply find another source of information. Rather than attempting to hide death from children, we should discuss it openly, honestly, and naturally.

Children obviously do not understand death the same way adults do. The concept develops gradually over time as children learn, grow, and experience life. When teaching them about the cycle of life, we must tailor the information to their individual needs.

In closing, I'd like to again commend you on your decision to take on the challenge of teaching children about death. I leave you with a final question. Would you feel comfortable if a child approached you today with questions about death, or would you prefer that she ask someone else? It is my sincere hope that you are now better prepared to educate the children you encounter, and that you find it easier to respond to their questions and facilitate their grief.

May you be rewarded in your efforts as you continue on life's journey.

A Tribute to Molly

Molly was a very special young lady. I had the privilege of knowing her for almost three years. During that time, Molly became much more than a patient to me; she became my friend. I first met Molly on the day of her diagnosis, and I was with her at the moment of her death. It was a profound experience.

One of the first things I realized about Molly was that she was not a complainer. No matter how much she was hurting or how miserable she felt, she rarely complained. She took everything in stride. I was continually amazed at her courage and strength.

The disease took so much from Molly. She lost the security of her health, the routine of day-to-day life, and the childhood innocence that believes Mom and Dad can somehow make everything all better. She lost her hair, her leg, a lung, and ultimately her life. Yet through it all she remained strong, even until the moment of death. Molly taught me that no matter how difficult a situation might seem, there is always something to be gained from it if only we have the courage to look for and find it.

About a week before her death, I asked Molly how she wanted to be remembered. She said, "As a fighter. I never gave up." I asked her if she understood that when she became a hospice patient she was still not giving up. She said, "Yes," and then she looked me right in the eye and said, almost angrily, "Why? Don't you think I'm still fighting?" I replied, "Oh, Molly. Yes! I know you are. You've always amazed me by your ability to bounce back from everything."

I remember how quickly Molly was up and getting about following her amputation. Pain had always been an issue for Molly, and yet it never stopped her. She continually picked herself up and moved forward. Her last autumn, after a little over a year of remission, Molly returned to the hospital. The disease had spread to her lung. When I talked to Molly about this, she said, "I know if it came back this once, it'll probably come back again, and I'll have to go through this [thoracotomy, an incision of the chest wall] all over again." The thought of that really scared her, and yet several months later she came back again for another thoracotomy. At that time it was necessary to remove the lung. Molly was faced with what was probably the most difficult decision of her life: Did she want to begin treatment again, or did she feel it was time to stop?

Molly knew that even with treatment she had almost no chance of buying herself any additional time. And she knew that more treatment would mean time in the hospital, away from home, and that she would be very sick. She made the decision not to begin treatment again. She chose, rather, to return home to be with her family. She wanted to live and enjoy the time that was left to her—and enjoy it she did. On the Thursday before her death, she went shopping with her mom (one of her favorite things to do). On Friday, she went to a movie with her family. Even as she was dying, Molly was living fully. Molly was Molly.

As difficult as some moments of her final days were, Molly continued to be concerned about others. She wasn't quite ready to die, and she needed to continue to give to others as she always had. Her family reassured her that she didn't have to be strong for them, that she could rest. But it wasn't her time yet. Molly wasn't ready. She needed to fight for life just a little bit longer.

By Monday night Molly was ready to die. She had fought a long, hard battle with cancer; and now she was ready for it to be over. She looked at each of us, and her final words were: "I love you, Dad. I love you, Jason. I love you, Mom. And I love you, Theresa." With that, Molly turned her head and died. It could not have been more beautiful. Molly was now at peace. She would struggle no more, and there would be no more pain.

I'll miss you, Molly—goodbye.

For Further Reading

To Read with Kids

Nadia the Willful by Sue Alexander (New York: Knopf, 1992)

When I Die, Will I Get Better? by Joeri and Piet Breebaart (New York: Peter Bedrick Books, 1993)

When Dinosaurs Die: A Guide to Understanding Death by Laurie Krasny Brown (Boston: Little Brown & Co., 1998)

The Fall of Freddie the Leaf: A Story of Life for All Ages by Leo F. Buscaglia (Austin, Tex.: Holt, Rinehart and Winston, 1983)

When Someone Dies by Sharon Greenlee (Atlanta: Peachtree Publishers, 1992)

What on Earth Do You Do When Someone Dies? by Trevor Romain (Minneapolis: Free Spirit Publishing, 1999)

Badger's Parting Gifts by Susan Varley (New York: Mulberry Books, 1992)

The Tenth Good Thing about Barney by Judith Viorst (New York: Atheneum, 1971)

I'll Always Love You by Hans Wilhelm (New York: Crown Pub., 1989)

Death of a Sibling

Goodbye Rune by Marit Kaldhol (Brooklyn, N. Y.: Kane/Miller Book Pub., 1987)

Losing Someone You Love: When a Brother or Sister Dies by Elizabeth Richter (New York: Putnam Pub. Group, 1986)

A Birthday Present for Daniel: A Child's Story of Loss by Juliet Cassuto Rothman (Amherst, N. Y.: Prometheus Books, 1996)

The Empty Place: A Child's Guide through Grief by Roberta Temes (New York: New Horizon Press, 1992)

Death of a Parent

When Your Parent Dies by Ron Klug (Minneapolis: Augsburg Fortress Publishers, 2001)

How it Feels When a Parent Dies by Jill Krementz (New York: Knopf, 1988)

The Rag Coat by Lauren Mills (Boston: Little Brown & Co., 1991)

Geranium Morning by E. Sandy Powell (Minneapolis: Carolrhoda Books, 1990)

Death of a Child

When the Bough Breaks: Forever after the Death of a Son or Daughter by Judith R. Bernstein (Kansas City, Mo.: Andrews McMeel Publishing, 1998)

When Goodbye Is Forever: Learning to Live Again after the Loss of a Child by John Bramblett (New York: Ballantine Books, 1991)

After the Death of a Child: Living with Loss through the Years by Ann K. Finkbeiner (Baltimore: Johns Hopkins Univ. Press, 1998)

Death Be Not Proud: A Memoir by John Gunther (New York: Harper Perennial, 1998)

When Your Child Dies by Theresa M. Huntley (Minneapolis: Augsburg Fortress Publishers, 2001)

Children Die, Too by Joy and Dr. S. M. Johnson (Omaha: Centering Corp., 1992)

A Broken Heart Still Beats: After Your Child Dies by Anne McCracken and Mary Semel (Center City, Minn.: Hazelden Information Education, 2000)

The Bereaved Parent by Harriet Sanoff Schiff (New York: Viking Press, 1978)

The Andrew Poems by Shelly Wagner (Lubbock, Tex.: Texas Tech. Univ. Press, 1994)

For Parents and Education Professionals

Life and Loss: A Guide to Help Grieving Children by Linda Goldman (New York: Brunner/Mazel, 1999)

Bereaved Children and Teens: A Support Guide for Parents and Professionals by Earl V. Grollman (Boston: Beacon Press, 1996)

When Your Child Loses a Loved One by Theresa M. Huntley (Minneapolis: Augsburg Fortress Publishers, 2001)

Keys to Helping Children Deal with Death and Grief by Joy Johnson (Hauppauge, N. Y.: Barrons Educational Series, 1999)

Helping Children Cope with the Loss of a Loved One: A Guide for Grownups by William C. Kroen (Minneapolis: Free Spirit Publishing, 1996)

On Children and Death: How Children and Their Parents Can and Do Cope with Death by Elisabeth Kübler-Ross (New York: Collier, 1997)

When Bad Things Happen to Good People by Rabbi Harold Kushner (New York: Schocken Books, 1989)

Parental Loss of a Child by Therese A. Rando (Champaign, Ill.: Research Press, 1986)

The Gift of a Memory by Marianne Richmond (Minneapolis: Waldman House Press, 2000)

The Worst Loss: How Families Heal from the Death of a Child by Barbara D. Rosof (New York: Henry Holt, 1995)

How to Survive the Loss of a Child: Filling the Emptiness and Rebuilding Your Life by Catherine M. Sanders (Roseville, Calif.: Prima Publishing, 1998)

Good Grief by Granger E. Westberg (Minneapolis: Augsburg Fortress Publishers, 2000)

Healing a Child's Grieving Heart by Alan D. Wolfelt (Laguna Hills, Calif.: Companion Press, 2001)

Hope and Healing

Remembering with Love: Messages of Hope for the First Year of Grieving and Beyond by Elizabeth Levang, Ph.D. and Sherokee Ilse (Minneapolis: Fairview Press, 1995)

Gentle Closings: How to Say Goodbye to Someone You Love by Ted Menten (Philadelphia, Pa.: Running Press, 1992)

Other Resources from Augsburg

Remembering Mama by Dara Dokas
32 pages, 0-8066-4352-8

A young girl expresses emotions connected with the loss of her mother and uses memories to work through her grief.

When Your Child Dies by Theresa M. Huntley
48 pages, 0-8066-4261-0

Offering grieving parents honest, practical guidance, Theresa Huntley gives insights into the grief process and the tasks of mourning. This book will help parents come to understand, accept, and live with their loss.

Good Grief
by Granger E. Westberg
64 pages, 0-8006-1114-4

Since its first edition in 1962, *Good Grief* has become a standard resource for people grieving losses. Westberg gently guides the reader through the stages of grief.

When Your Child Loses a Loved One
by Theresa M. Huntley
56 pages, 0-8066-4262-9

The author presents the guidance parents need to help their children grieve. Huntley explains how children understand death, how they grieve, and what steps help them understand and live with their loss.

Available wherever books are sold.